THE NEW MERMAIDS

The Country Wife

THE NEW MERMAIDS

General Editors
PHILIP BROCKBANK
Professor of English, University of York

BRIAN MORRIS
Professor of English, University of Sheffield

The Country Wife

WILLIAM WYCHERLEY

Edited by JOHN DIXON HUNT

ERNEST BENN LIMITED
LONDON & TONBRIDGE

First published in this form 1973
by Ernest Benn Limited
Sovereign Way · Tonbridge · Kent &
25 New Street Square · Fleet Street · London · EC4A 3JA

© *Ernest Benn Limited 1973*

Distributed in Canada by
The General Publishing Company Limited · Toronto

Printed in Great Britain
ISBN 0 510-34351-1
Paperback 0 510-34352-x

CONTENTS

ACKNOWLEDGEMENTS

In editing the text I have made use of four modern editions of the play: those by Montague Summers, *The Complete Works of William Wycherley*, 4 vols. (London, 1924); by Ursula Todd-Naylor, *Smith College Studies in Modern Languages*, XII (Northampton, Mass., 1930–31); by Thomas H. Fujimura in the Regents Restoration Drama Series (London, 1965); and by Gerald Weales, *The Complete Plays of William Wycherley*, Anchor Books (New York, 1966). Some further collation has enabled me to add a few variants.

I am also grateful for suggestions and comments during my work to my colleague Michael Cordner and to Brian Morris, 'nostrorum sermonum candide iudex'.

York   J.D.H.
June 1972

INTRODUCTION

THE AUTHOR

William Wycherley, the eldest son of Daniel Wycherley, a Shropshire gentleman, was born in the winter of 1640 at Clive, a village twelve miles north of Shrewsbury. He was educated at home by his father, an intelligent man but with a logical mind and meticulous method that seemed to delight most in the constant litigation in which he engaged. From this stern, even dour, domestic *regimen*, William Wycherley was sent at about the age of fifteen to be educated in France, where he spent several years in the vicinity of the Charente. He became acquainted here with Julie de Montausier, a celebrated figure of the French *salons*, who was perhaps responsible for his conversion to Catholicism but, more importantly, must have promoted Wycherley's general education by her fascinating and intellectual presence. In 1660 he returned to England and entered Queen's College, Oxford, as a gentleman commoner. His sojourn there was short—'he wore not a gown'—and he left without a degree and with only a resumption of his Protestant faith to mark his time there. In November 1660 he entered the Inner Temple.

Though not entirely neglecting his legal studies, he began to lead the fashionable life of a wit about town. In 1665 he fought in the Second Dutch War at the battle where the Duke of York defeated Opdam, celebrated both in Dryden's *Annus Mirabilis* and in Wycherley's own verses, '*On a sea fight which the author was in betwixt the* English *and* Dutch'. Wycherley first drew the attention of the town with a poem of 1669, *Hero and Leander in Burlesque*, but it was two years later that his first play, *Love In A Wood*, was performed at the Theatre Royal, Drury Lane. It brought him literary and social success: as Dennis said, 'he became acquainted with several of the most celebrated wits both of the Court and Town'.[1] It also procured him an intrigue with Barbara Palmer, Duchess of Cleveland and, through her, friendship with George Villiers, Duke of Buckingham.

A fire at the Theatre Royal in 1672 prevented Wycherley's second play, *The Gentleman Dancing-Master*, being performed there. It was offered instead in March at a rival theatre, the Dorset Garden, but—as the Prologue of *The Country Wife* testifies—was coolly received.

[1] Quoted Montague Summers, *The Complete Works of William Wycherley* (1924), I, 33, to which I am indebted for other biographical information in this introduction.

It was at the restored Drury Lane theatre and by the former company
that *The Country Wife* was offered in 1674/75, with much success.
In the words of his first biographer, Richardson Pack, he was henceforth

> not only courted by the men, but his person was as well received by
> the ladies; and as King Charles was extremely fond of him upon
> some account of his wit, some of the royal mistresses . . . set no less
> value upon these parts in him, of which they were more proper
> judges.

Wycherley lived now in the fashionable quarter, in Bow Street,
Covent Garden.

The winter of 1676 saw the equally successful production of his
next play, *The Plain Dealer*, but about a year afterwards Wycherley
became dangerously ill. His reputation was such that Charles II not
only visited his sickbed but urged him to winter in Montpellier and
provided £500 for the necessary expenses. He returned in 1679 and
with the king's favour still seeming to smile upon him was appointed
tutor to the king's illegitimate son, Charles Lennox, Duke of Rich-
mond, at a most substantial salary. But sometime in the summer of
that year he met at Tunbridge Wells Laetitia Isabella, widow of
Charles Moore, second Earl of Drogheda, whom he married
clandestinely either late in 1679 or early the next year. Troubles then
seem to have descended upon Wycherley: the king was displeased
that he had not been informed of the marriage and the tutorship was
revoked. The Countess of Drogheda proved so suspicious of all her
husband's actions that her jealousy provoked noisy recriminations
and constant spying upon Wycherley's movements. When she died
the following year, leaving him her entire fortune, the will was dis-
puted by her family and Wycherley was subjected to interminable
and complicated lawsuits which drained him of so much money that
—with no help forthcoming from either his father or Charles II—he
was thrown into the Fleet Prison for debt.

He remained there for several years and was eventually released
through the intervention of James II who had, according to tradition,
been delighted by a performance at Court in 1685 of *The Plain Dealer*
and, learning of its author's plight, offered to settle his debts. But
Wycherley apparently forbore to disclose the full extent of his
debts and even after his release was in severe financial straits. After
1688, with declining health as well as funds, he was forced to live at
Clive, with only occasional visits to London. After 1697 when he
inherited the family estates at his father's death, he was able to
return to live in London. He became something of a literary legend,
pointed out to visitors at the coffee houses and courted by such
young writers as Alexander Pope, whose help was sought in revising
and correcting some of Wycherley's manuscript verses.

On 20 December 1715—perhaps to spite a troublesome nephew upon whom the estate was entailed—Wycherley married again, with the result that at his death eleven days later (during the night of 31 December 1715/1 January 1716) his young widow (the former Elizabeth Jackson) was left £400 a year which the nephew was obliged to pay. Though he died a Catholic—Macaulay suggested that the patronage of James II, himself a Catholic, may have occasioned this reconversion—Wycherley was buried in the vault of St Paul's, Covent Garden.

THE PLAY

The Country Wife was first performed on Tuesday 12 January 1674/75,[2] and again three days later. It was entered in the *Stationers' Register* the day following the first performance, listed in the *Term Catalogues* on 10 May 1675, and also published that year. It was revived in the repertory the following year and there seem to have been further revivals at the time of the later editions—1683, 1688, and 1695. It continued to be performed during the eighteenth century. From 1765, as the second half of double bills, was offered a farce in two acts, entitled *The Country-Wife*, adapted by John Lee from Wycherley's play. If Lee eliminated Horner and the Fidgets, Garrick's adaptation of 1766—*The Country Girl*—went even further: names were changed (Horner becomes Belville!) and the episodes of Horner's stratagem eliminated. One of Wycherley's modern editors calls it 'this eviscerated and offensive caricature of Wycherley's comedy' and also cites Moore's 'greasy' apophthegm: 'Though the very rinsings of Wycherley's play has [*sic*] a raciness in them that is indestructible, yet *The Country Girl* hangs flat on the palate after the other'.[3] Nevertheless it was Garrick's version that was played throughout the nineteenth century until, in 1924, *The Country Wife* resumed its career on the English stage.

It is generally assumed that Wycherley was influenced by two Molière plays in writing *The Country Wife*.[4] Certainly, some incidents were probably borrowed from *L'École des maris* and *L'École des femmes*, such as the mistaken delivery of a letter to the lover of the bearer's fiancée or the use of disguise by a woman to escape domestic imprisonment. But the tone of the two dramatists is considerably different: it is a question not only of the temper or tone of their

[2] *The London Stage 1660–1800*, ed. William Van Lennep (Carbondale, Ill., 1965), I, 227.

[3] Summers, op. cit., II, 7.

[4] Various passages from the French for comparison with Wycherley may be found below, pp. xxi ff.

satire, but of the dramatic texture, itself a mirror of different social and cultural tones. These can both perhaps be seen best in a comparison of Arnolphe's praise of a silly wife (see below, p. xxii) with the *dialogue* where Pinchwife is teased by Horner, Dorilant, and Harcourt about his country wife.

The other famous 'source' for Wycherley's play is Terence's *Eunuchus*. But it is here that Wycherley himself leads us from literary archaeology to criticism—in the motto on the title-page and perhaps in Horner's '*Probatum est*' of the first scene (I.i, 163) we are reminded that it is less the provenance of an idea than its new life that warrants attention.

In a recent Sunday colour supplement eminent ladies were asked to name the man they thought most 'manly' and the one who chose Horner commented that the 'very word "manliness" causes me to feel queasy. It implies physical and mental boneheadedness, combined with a certain inept fraudulence'. This goes some way towards defining the peculiar quality of the first scene between Horner and the Quack. The ruthless and totally efficient mentality that Horner (the name is no accident, nor its double meaning) brings to the task of catering for his sexual appetites is Wycherley's characteristic contribution to Terence's device. The self-respect that one supposes most males would preserve in public about their virility is sacrificed for the private satisfaction of encounters with women. No wonder the Quack needs convincing of the effectiveness of Horner's scheme. Horner's single-mindedness, the cool calculation of his conduct, marks him as a peculiarly compelling spokesman of a certain Restoration egotism, what Clarendon identified as everyone doing 'that which was good in his own eyes'.[5] The success of his scheme, at least from one viewpoint, is measured by the dance of cuckolds at the end—as it were, all his own work.

The Restoration saw much consideration of the proper function and role of the hero and the heroic, and it is worth examining Horner briefly in this context. Perhaps it is no accident that in the years after 1688 London talk had it that Wycherley would collaborate with Dryden on a new play, for some aspects of the latter's heroes jibe with certain of Horner's qualities. The 'libertine hero' of Restoration comedy flourished at the same time as Dryden was writing his rhymed, heroic plays and, as Arthur Kirsch has remarked,

> to the people who saw or read them at the time the theatrical appeal of comedy and tragedy was usually very similar and their moral assumptions seemed compatible. The opposition between an allegedly romantic heroic drama and a realistic comedy of manners,

[5] Quoted John Barnard, 'Drama from the Restoration till 1710,' *English Drama to 1710*, ed. C. Ricks (1971), p. 379.

the heroes of the former ideal and idealized, the heroes of the latter natural and naturalistic, is a modern and tendentious distinction.[6]

Kirsch then continues with a libertine interpretation of Dryden's plays. If that critical process is reversed, Horner may be seen to borrow some of the charisma of the heroes of *Tyrannick Love* or *The Conquest of Granada*. If Dryden's heroes were in debt to the code of manners by which some of his audience lived, then Horner shares the morality that Dryden, in his preface to *The Conquest of Granada*, said he wished to manifest in his heroic plays: 'what men of great spirits would certainly do, when they were provok'd, not what they were obliged to do by the strict rules of moral vertue'. And it is evident that Horner's heroic stature in such amoral enterprises is less bathetic than is implied by a contemporary sceptic of the heroic drama, writing in 1673:

> I have known a little Hector, more to glory in the sleights he is capable of using in picking up a Wench, and in the variety of his knowledge, than a great Captain ever did, in the stratagems and policies of War: the desire of glory and singularity is now as violent as ever, though its satisfaction is placed in such trifling and idle acquirements . . .

In comparison with Pinchwife, whose speech, it has been noted,[7] is littered with quasi-heroic images and who twice draws his sword, Horner's heroism is far more substantial and achieved. His libertine accomplishments throughout the play are magnificent by the standards not only of his own sexual egotism (by which we cannot avoid occasionally judging him) but also of a large proportion of those husbands and wives he deceives. Yet this 'heroic' quality in his character consorts closely with those elements that Wycherley seems to use to define his basic vulnerability.

But the measure of Horner's failure is not that of the writer of 1673 who regretted satisfaction 'placed in such trifling and idle acquirements'. That is the morality of the old Puritan antagonism to the stage, which Wycherley, delighting in and using the theatre so brilliantly, would not share. He locates his reservations rather in what one might identify as the paradoxical disadvantages of a Hobbesian ethic, most remarkably and penetratingly explored in the Restoration by some of Rochester's poems.

[6] *Dryden's Heroic Drama* (Princeton, 1965), p. 35. I am indebted generally to Mr Kirsch's book in this section of my discussion.

[7] Norman N. Holland, *The First Modern Comedies* (Cambridge, Mass., 1959), p. 74. Holland also suggests (p. 85), though I am more sceptical, that Horner's 'castration' may be seen as an heroic 'wound of love'; yet, if this were so, it would serve to focus both the heroic and the reductive capabilities of Horner.

In the *Leviathan* Hobbes celebrates the notion that surely sustains many heroes of Restoration comedy and tragedy:

> Joy, arising from imagination of a man's own power and ability, is that exultation of the mind which is called Glorying, for the general inclination of all mankind [is] a perpetual and restless desire of power after power, that closeth only in death.[8]

The sexual pun (unintended by Hobbes) on 'death' makes that remark even more apt for Restoration characters like Horner. 'Man's own power and ability' in sexual matters, the 'glory' of his powerful appetite, is the theme of much of Horner's career, as of Rochester's poetry. The premise of their heroic activity in boudoir and bed is the immorality of the natural world:

> Since 'tis nature's law to change
> Constancy alone is strange.[9]

Rochester's poetic *persona* argues wittily that it is necessary to leave his mistress in order to encourage her huge ambitions:

> See, the kind seed-receiving earth
> To every grain affords a birth.
> On her no showers unwelcome fall;
> Her willing womb retains 'em all.
>> And shall my Celia be confined?
>> No! Live up to thy mighty mind,
>> And be the mistress of mankind. (p. 81)

This whoredom of nature authorizes the nightly charade beneath the pastoral trees of St James's Park:

> Each imitative branch does twine
> In some loved fold of Aretine,
> And nightly now beneath their shade
> Are buggeries, rapes, and incests made.
> Unto this all-sin-sheltering grove
> Whores of the bulk and the alcove,
> Great ladies, chambermaids, and drudges,
> The ragpicker, and heiress trudges.
> Carmen, divines, great lords, and tailors,
> Prentices, poets, pimps, and jailers,
> Footmen, fine fops do here arrive,
> And here promiscuously they swive. (p. 41)

The fashion in which Rochester implies his satire of such sexual

[8] Quoted Barnard, op. cit., p. 386
[9] *The Complete Poems of John Wilmot, Earl of Rochester*, ed. David M. Vieth (New Haven and London, 1968), p. 8. All other references are to this edition.

excess is not through any direct appeal to some absolute moral
standard that somehow transcends even natural law: 'A Satyr against
Reason and Mankind' should remind us of that—

> Reason, an *ignis fatuus* in the mind,
> Which, leaving light of nature, sense, behind,
> Pathless and dangerous wandering ways it takes
> Through error's fenny bogs and thorny brakes. (p. 95)

So it is not by reason that Rochester enforces any moral perspectives,
but by elaborating his picture of a world obsessed with the senses
until we are able to see its grotesque distortions.[10] Sexual man in
Rochester's vision—whether it be Fair Chloris masturbating in the
pigsty or the disabled debauchee turned *voyeur*—forces himself to a
tragic absurdity in the pursuit of pleasure and so provides the poet
with irrefutable evidence for his conclusion that 'Man differs more
from man, than man from beast' (p. 101).

Wycherley's Horner, exhausted by his exploits in the china
closet,[11] may also be seen as the victim of a total dedication to
sensual pleasure. The grotesque, even unpleasant, undertones of
these later scenes with his cohorts of women—especially the drunken
scene—are enforced also by the equally grotesque distortions of idea
and language that Horner's conduct engineers. Lady Fidget's
response to being told by Horner of his 'device' sets the tenor of this
decadence:

> could you be so generous, so truly a man of honour, as for the sakes of
> us women of honour . . . (II.i, 522–3)

'Generosity' and 'honour', like reason or love in Rochester, are forced
into reductive meanings. So it is with a fine dramatic irony that
Wycherley has Horner express his contempt for Sparkish in a
denunciation of 'all that force nature, and would be still what she
forbids 'em' (I. i, 249–50). For Horner is himself the most extreme
forcer of nature, not only in the sense of an exaggeration of one
natural urge, but in the suppression of any rival instincts that would
distract from that single purpose. When he boasts that the town has
'such variety of dainties that we are seldom hungry' (I. i, 373–4) he
declares his own commitment to appetite; and in the ironic posturing
of his 'castration' he acts the part of one for whom 'Good fellowship
and friendship are lasting, rational, and manly pleasures' (I.i, 193–4)
—in other words, he himself doesn't really care a whit for them. He
can profess a momentary sorrow for a friend's misfortune—'Poor
Harcourt! I am sorry thou hast missed her' (IV. iii, 372–3)—though the

[10] See Ronald Berman, 'Rochester and the Defeat of the Senses,' *The
Kenyon Review*, XXVI (1964), 354 *et seq*.
[11] Both Horner's exhaustion and his rapid recovery were apparently em-
phasized—and rightly—at the 1969 Chichester Festival production, where
the part was played by Keith Baxter.

aside could equally lament the frustration of a fellow libertine. More usually his cynical realism can envisage only one role for friendship—cheating one's country acquaintances. The crudity of much of his wit—the often transparent *double-entendres*—and what Macaulay generally recognized as Wycherley's indecencies serve to endorse this reductive vision. It is as much an index of Horner's insufficiency as of his mastery.

Horner's heroic endeavours, then, are inseparable from his almost horrifying single-mindedness. Similarly, the means by which he becomes the vehicle of Wycherley's satire of society's gullibility and hypocrisy is also, by its extraordinary thoroughness of motive and method, how Wycherley suggests that Horner becomes his own victim. We laugh as a result of his first role, but the dramatic situation disguises perhaps how little we are secure in applauding his own situation. (It is interesting to contrast Rochester here, where the absence of such a dramatic context allows the tragic insufficiency of a total dedication to pleasure to be appreciated more readily.) Horner is certainly a highly successful vehicle for exposing both Sir Jaspar's credulity and the unabashed appetite of such as Lady Fidget—'O filthy French beast! foh, foh! Why do we stay? . . . I can't endure the sight of him' (I. i, 101–2). The more horrifying the society he exposes, the more heroic his stance might appear: 'plain dealing is a jewel' (IV. iii, 112) *indeed*. But we appreciate less readily than we might, I think, the consequences to Horner himself of his programme. Yet we are reminded often enough of what he has irretrievably sacrificed to his ambitions—as he himself acknowledges: 'for in these cases I am still on the criminal's side, against the innocent' (V. iv, 223–4). His own implied addition to the alchemy of sexual experiment (I. i, 145) may also suggest his ultimate failure to find that particular philosopher's stone. As with Rochester's Celia, whose ambition to be the 'mistress of mankind' may (even with world enough and time) prove a crippling endeavour, so Horner's enterprise is ultimately as criminal as it is heroic.

The society that Horner exposes is, as one of its prime citizens remarks, 'a nasty world' (II. i, 337). Frankness, here, is only gullible stupidity; hypocrisy is the sustaining energy that alternates with sexual desire—either the butler is lovely in Mrs Squeamish's eyes (V. iv, 49) or Lady Fidget exclaims 'O lord, here's a man! Sir Jaspar, my mask, my mask!' (IV. iii, 228); ceremony in 'love and eating is as ridiculous as in fighting' (V. iv, 86); and these reductive assumptions contaminate the whole of society:

> Our virtue is like the statesman's religion, the Quaker's word, the gamester's oath, and the great man's honour—but to cheat those that trust us. (V. iv, 100–103)

In a world where wives are seen as cash, freehold, or haberdashery, marriage is obviously either a precarious institution or one of mere graceless habit—'the same indifferency and ill-breeding as if we were all married to 'em' (II. i, 347–8). Horner's exposure of these frightening abysses has a direct bearing upon one of Wycherley's main concerns in the play—marriage. And we see the interconnection of these various concerns in the scene in the New Exchange.

We are offered three principal marital situations to contemplate—those of the Pinchwifes, the Fidgets, and the proposed match between Alithea and Sparkish. Sir Jaspar Fidget is more concerned with his own business about the town than with his wife; his particular form of solicitude towards her—'as much a husband's prudence to provide innocent diversion for a wife as to hinder her unlawful pleasures' (I. i, 116–18)—is highly susceptible to Horner's exploitation of him. Like most of the characters in the play his conduct of human relations is based upon outward appearances[12]—it is surely important that at his first entrance into Horner's lodgings he should be seen to be looking for outward and visible signs of Horner's 'condition': Horner tells the Quack as much when (I.i, 129–30) he says Sir Jaspar will believe 'the report and *my carriage*'. It is perhaps a further irony that in this case Sir Jaspar should have believed what he saw—nothing.

It is perhaps worth asking, parenthetically, at this point whether Wycherley expected us to believe that the town would credit Horner's story, whether the device was lent some local credence by current gossip, or whether—if not too subtle an argument—the medical implausibility of Horner's tale is designed to draw our attention to the degree of gullibility manifested by people like Sir Jaspar.

By one of the fine dramatic contrivances of the play Pinchwife never learns until the very end about Horner's 'condition'. He is a man who thinks he knows the town—and it is again ironic that his judgement of Horner throughout the play certainly endorses that. But he is out-manoeuvred by a man who knows it better and who can take advantage of its social insecurities. When Steele saw *The Country Wife* in 1709 he wrote of Pinchwife that he

> is represented to be one of those debauchees who run through the vices of the Town, and believe, when they think fit, they can marry and settle at their ease. His own knowledge of the Iniquity of the Age makes him choose a Wife wholly ignorant of it, and place his security in her want of skill to abuse him.[13]

[12] As Holland (op. cit., p. 81) remarks, these outward pretences have become so inbred that they are maintained even in the most absurd situations, such as when Lady Fidget is about to yield to Horner.

[13] *The Tatler* of 16 April; quoted also by Summers, op. cit., II, 5.

Pinchwife's attitudes in marriage, however, are still those of the town libertine: since he 'could never keep a whore to' himself (I. i, 429–30), he tries to keep a wife and his jealousy not only attracts more attention to Margery but also, like Sir Jaspar's 'prudence', is an apt instrument of Horner's stratagems against him.

Pinchwife's prescription for a safe marriage, which at least according to the town wits is none at all, is to remove Margery to the country. (One is reminded of Rochester, bitten by a dog, hoping that it was no worse than to be married and live in the country.[14]) But such country emprisonments are no positive contribution to marital felicity, as Alithea sharply remarks:

> she is sent into the country, which is the last ill usage of a husband to a wife, I think. (IV.i, 59–61)

As that confident metropolitan pronouncement and its context suggest, Alithea is no simple heroine and those critics who see her and Harcourt as the standard by which Wycherley intends the other marriages to be judged miss much in her character. For one thing, though, like Pinchwife, she professes to know the ways of the town, she is absurdly deceived in Sparkish, mistaking an outward virtue— absence of jealousy—for an inward strength. It is absurd not least because even if the outward virtue were real and strong, it is so evidently supported by no other. It crumbles easily and on account of mistaken evidence—so we have a further ironic example of somebody being right all along despite appearances or gossip to the contrary.

Sparkish is marrying Alithea for the money (£5,000), as he himself admits: 'I might have married your portion' (V. iii, 68). No other personal consideration bothers him or distracts from his foolish aping of urban sophistication. Yet it is a curious feature of his role in the play that despite the affectations and pretensions he stumbles upon truths about human relationships that the other more intelligent characters do not. Consider:

> (*to Alithea*) That he makes love to you is a sign you are handsome; and that I am not jealous is a sign you are virtuous. That, I think, is for your honour. (III. ii, 210–13)
> (*to Pinchwife*) Are you not ashamed that I should have more confidence in the chastity of your family than you have? (III. ii, 331–2)

In comparison, Harcourt's 'he wants . . . jealousy, the only infallible sign' (II. i, 214–15) of love seems a little too worldly and simplistic. Yet Sparkish has insufficient intelligence to register his own perceptions and it is Harcourt who finally triumphs with Alithea. Even in this

---

[14] Cited by Ursula Todd-Naylor in the introduction to her edition of the play (see below, p. xxv), p. xxxiv.

potentially sentimental victory of true love—Harcourt at the end wants to marry her despite the apparent betrayal of her innocence to Horner—we are surely not allowed to have complete confidence.

One critic talks of the 'enduring social forms' into which Alithea's, but not Margery's, love is channelled.[15] Certainly, as Alithea remarks of Sparkish in the Second Act, 'love proceeds from esteem' (II. i, 216), a sentiment that properly sustains Harcourt's final profession of love. And she appears to give Harcourt, unlike Sparkish, her 'heart' together with her 'person'. But I can forget neither her addiction to Sparkish, nor her final *volte-face*, at which Sparkish retorts 'I see virtue makes a woman as troublesome as a little reading or learning'; (III. ii, 239–40), nor the inefficacy of Harcourt's honesty. His role as curate is neither well sustained nor instrumental, in effect, in furthering his own cause; he succeeds with Alithea really through no actions of his own. So, just as we must not neglect our delight and entertainment in face of the absurdities of the Pinchwife and Fidget *ménages*, while attending to their often appalling humanity, so we should retain some scepticism while contemplating the final idyll of the man who proclaims that 'I edify, madam, so much that I am impatient' (V. iv, 380) to be a husband.

With the Country Wife herself Wycherley's concern with marriage and his satiric use of Horner coincide. Her initial innocence of town manners and customs is matched by the openness and absence of any pretence in Horner's seduction of her. They make an apt couple, sharing a zestful sexual appetite, he because he has excluded all other possibilities, she because that is all she cares for: it is typical both of her lustful nature and of her ignorance of town arts that she enjoys the actors because they are fine figures of men. Her naivety, like Horner's grotesque sexual dedication, serves to satirize the sophisticated and hypocritical manners of those around her, including those of her absurdly jealous husband. Her country conduct and assumptions—Hampshire seems to have been regarded as the epitome of provincial backwaters—call into question much that the worldly folk of the play take for granted. Her surprise at writing letters to people in the same town, her marvellous ignorance about cuckold's signs or marrying Horner ('Don't I see every day at London here, women leave their first husbands, and go and live with other men as their wives?'; V. iv, 208–10), her curiosity about 'jealousy' —these all serve to show up the absurdities of town life.

Yet Margery offers no positive mode of conduct herself and her innocence is swiftly compounded with (one cannot really talk of corrupted by) the libertine *mores* of the town. Even as she succumbs to them, she serves to illustrate their hollowness. In his efforts to conceal her from the town, Pinchwife teaches her precisely those

[15] Holland, op. cit., p. 82.

devices—disguise and letter-writing—by which the town furthers its desires. Her disguise (as Alithea) and Horner's (as a eunuch) success-fully complement each other. Steele thought Margery was a woman without skill: if she is in the first scene, it is a deficiency that she quickly remedies and by the final scene we are given the spectacle of her learning from the entire company the ultimate skill—that of lying. With her simple rural faith in fertility and virility she would jump to rescue Horner's reputation, having only a short while before experienced his full sexual powers: but she is prevailed upon to substantiate the fiction of Horner's 'condition'. Doubtless, her letters will soon be full of their 'flames, darts, fates, destinies' (IV. iii, 349) if they too will ensure her continued sexual satisfaction. Margery is indeed 'the worse for your town documents' (II. i, 54).

The Restoration and early eighteenth century made much of the rivalries between town and country. Wycherley—with memories of his home education at Clive to contrast with his life in France and London—could hardly be expected to betray the town. Yet his por-trait of Margery, though she is according to her husband as well as Steele 'ill-bred' in the country, furnishes a resonant critique of those town people who depend, in Harcourt's words, upon being 'the contraries to that they would seem' (I. i, 251). Together with Horner she is used by Wycherley to savage the obsessions and deceits (in-cluding self-deceits) of his age. Wycherley is, then, not entirely of the company of those playwrights whom Dorilant defends because they 'must follow their copy—the age' (III. ii, 120). He would agree with Sparkish—his own portrait in this volume testifies to that agreement —that 'painters don't draw the smallpox or pimples in one's face' (III. ii, 129–30). But his own special vision required a grotesque art that he blended subtly with the heroic expectations of his audience. Horner, acting his part, tells Dorilant that he hates women 'and would hate 'em yet more, I'll frequent 'em' (III. ii, 16–17). It is the play's mastery that Horner himself, as well as the audience, comes to realize the absolute truth of that unintended perception.

COMPARISONS WITH MOLIERE

(Text and references are from *Oeuvres Complètes*, I, Bibliothèque de la Pléiade, Paris, 1956)

LÉONOR
    Voyez-vous Isabelle avec nous à regret?
SGANARELLE
    Oui, vous me la gâtez, puisqu'il faut parler net.
    Vos visites ici ne font que me déplaire,
    Et vous m'obligerez de ne nous en plus faire.
LÉONOR
    Voulez-vous que mon coeur vous parle net aussi?
    J'ignore de quel oeil elle voit tout ceci;
    Mais je sais ce qu'en moi ferait la défiance;
    Et quoiqu'un même sang nous ait donné naissance,
    Nous sommes bien peu soeurs s'il faut que chaque jour
    Vos manières d'agir lui donnent de l'amour.
LISETTE
    En effet, tous ces soins sont des choses infâmes.
    Sommes-nous chez les Turcs pour renfermer les femmes?
    Car on dit qu'on les tient esclaves en ce lieu,
    Et que c'est pour cela qu'ils sont maudits de Dieu.
    Notre honneur est, Monsieur, bien sujet à faiblesse,
    S'il faut qu'il ait besoin qu'on le garde sans cesse.
    Pensez-vous, après tout, que ces précautions
    Servent de quelque obstacle à nos intentions,
    Et quand nous nous mettons quelque chose à la tête,
    Que l'homme le plus fin ne soit pas une bête?
    Toutes ces gardes-là sont visions de fous:
    Le plus sûr est, ma foi, de se fier en nous.
    Qui nous gêne se met en un péril extrême,
    Et toujours notre honneur veut se garder lui-même.
    C'est nous inspirer presque un désir de pécher,
    Que montrer tant de soins de nous en empêcher;
    Et si par un mari je me voyais contrainte,
    J'aurais fort grande pente à confirmer sa crainte.
            (Molière, *L'École des maris*, I.ii., pp. 350–1)

Compare scene between Pinchwife and Alithea, II.i, 36 ff.

ARNOLPHE
> Épouser une sotte est pour n'être point sot.
> Je crois, en bon chrétien, votre moitié fort sage;
> Mais une femme habile est un mauvais présage,
> Et je sais ce qu'il coûte à de certaines gens
> Pour avoir pris les leurs avec trop de talens.
> Moi, j'irais me charger d'une spirituelle
> Qui ne parlerait rien que cercle et que ruelle,
> Qui de prose et de vers ferait de doux écrits,
> Et que visiteraient marquis et beaux esprits,
> Tandis que, sous le nom de mari de Madame,
> Je serais comme un saint que pas un ne réclame?
> Non, non, je ne veux point d'un esprit qui soit haut;
> Et femme qui compose en sait plus qu'il ne faut.
> Je prétends que la mienne, en clartés peu sublime,
> Même ne sache pas ce que c'est qu'une rime;
> Et s'il faut qu'avec elle on joue au corbillon
> Et qu'on vienne à lui dire à son tour: 'Qu'y met-on?'
> Je veux qu'elle réponde: 'Une tarte à la crème';
> En un mot, qu'-elle soit d'une ignorance extrême;
> Et c'est assez pour elle, à vous en bien parler,
> De savoir prier Dieu, m'aimer, coudre et filer.

CHRYSALDE
> Une femme stupide est donc votre marotte?

ARNOLPHE
> Tant, que j'aimerais mieux une laide bien sotte
> Qu'une femme fort belle avec beaucoup d'esprit.
>   Molière, *L'École des femmes*, I.i., p. 448)

Compare scene between Pinchwife and his town 'friends', I.i, 335 ff.

ARNOLPHE
> Oui. Mais que faisait-il étant seul avec vous?

AGNÈS
> Il disait qu'il m'aimait d'une amour sans seconde,
> Et me disait des mots les plus gentils du monde,
> Des choses que jamais rien ne peut égaler,
> Et dont, toutes les fois que je l'entends parler,
> La douceur me chatouille et là dedans remue
> Certain je ne sais quoi dont je suis toute émue.

ARNOLPHE (*à part*)
> O facheux examen d'un mystère fatal,
> Où l'examinateur souffre seul tout le mal!

                                            (*A Agnès*)

Outre tous ces discours, toutes ces gentillesses,
Ne vous faisoit-il point aussi quelques caresses?
AGNÈS
Oh tant! Il me prenait et les mains et les bras,
Et de me les baiser il n'était jamais las.
ARNOLPHE
Ne vous a-t-il point pris, Agnès, quelque autre chose?
                              (*La voyant interdite*)
Ouf!
AGNÈS
       Hé! il m'a ...
ARNOLPHE
              Quoi?
AGNÈS
                   Pris ...
ARNOLPHE
                        Euh!
AGNÈS
                            Le ...
ARNOLPHE
                                Plaît-il?
AGNÈS
                                        Je n'ose,
Et vous vous fâcherez peut-être contre moi.
ARNOLPHE
              Non.
AGNÈS
                   Si fait.
ARNOLPHE
                        Mon Dieu, non!
AGNÈS
                                 Jurez donc votre foi.
ARNOLPHE
              Ma foi, soit.
AGNÈS
                   Il m'a pris ... Vous serez en colère.
ARNOLPHE
              Non.
AGNÈS
                   Si.
ARNOLPHE
                        Non, non, non, non. Diantre! que de mystère!
              Qu'est-ce qu'il vous a pris?
AGNÈS
                   Il ...

ARNOLPHE (*à part*)
> Je souffre en damné.

AGNÈS
> Il m'a pris le ruban que vous m'aviez donné.
> À vous dire le vrai, je n'ai pu m'en défendre.

ARNOLPHE (*reprenant haleine*)
> Passe pour le ruban. Mais je voulois apprendre
> S'il ne vous a rien fait que vous baiser les bras.

AGNÈS
> Comment? est-ce qu'on fait d'autres choses?

ARNOLPHE
> Non pas.
> Mais pour guérir du mal qu'il dit qui le possède,
> N'a-t-il point exigé de vous d'autre remède?

AGNÈS
> Non. Vous pouvez juger, s'il en eût demandé,
> Que pour le secourir j'aurais tout accordé.

> > (Molière, *L'École des femmes*, II,v., pp. 469–70)

Compare the scene between Pinchwife and Margery, IV.ii,
5 ff.

HORACE (*lit*)
'Je veux vous écrire, et je suis bien en peine par où je m'y prendrai. J'ai des pensées que je désirerais que vous sussiez; mais je ne sais comment faire pour vous les dire, et je me défie de mes paroles. Comme je commence à connaître qu'on m'a toujours tenue dans l'ignorance, j'ai peur de mettre quelque chose qui ne soit pas bien, et d'en dire plus que je ne devrais. En vérité, je ne sais ce que vous m'avez fait; mais je sens que je suis fâchée à mourir de ce qu'on me fait faire contre vous, que j'aurai toutes les peines du monde à me passer de vous, et que je serais bien aise d'être à vous. Peutêtre qu'il y a du mal à dire cela; mais enfin je ne puis m'empêcher de le dire, et je voudrois que cela se pût faire sans qu'il y en eût. On me dit fort que tous les jeunes hommes sont des trompeurs, qu'il ne les faut point écouter, et que tout ce que vous me dites n'est que pour m'abuser; mais je vous assure que je n'ai pu encore me figurer cela de vous, et je suis si touchée de vos paroles, que je ne saurais croire qu'elles soient menteuses. Dites-moi franchement ce qui en est; car enfin, comme je suis sans malice, vous auriez le plus grand tort du monde, si vous me trompiez; et je pense que j'en mourrais de déplaisir'.

> > (Molière, *L'École des femmes*, III,iv., p. 485)

Compare with Margery, IV.ii, 150–164.

NOTE ON THE TEXT

The Country Wife was first published in 1675 and it is upon this excellent original quarto (Q1) that the present edition is based: the copy text is the British Museum (C 34, 1 26). The next two editions of 1683 (Q2) and 1688 (Q3) correct some minor errors of Q1. Variants increase with Q4 (with *Country-Wife* in the running title) of 1695 and with Q5 (*Country Wife* in running title), also of 1695 and printed from Q4. On the relationship of these two texts of 1695 see the note by Robert N. E. Megaw in *Studies in Bibliography*, III, 252–3; I have accepted his conclusion that Q4 and Q5 are reversed in Gertrude L. Woodward and James G. McManaway, *A Check List of English Plays 1641–1700* (Chicago, 1945), p. 145. *The Country Wife* appeared once more during Wycherley's life, in the octavo of 1713, *The works of the ingenious Mr William Wycherley collected into one volume* (O).

The present text is modernized in spelling, and punctuation has been normalized with a view to clarifying Wycherley's rhetorical patterns for the modern reader. I have departed from the usual practice of the copy text and in speech prefixes dropped *Mr* from before *Pinchwife* to avoid any possibility of confusing him as speaker with *Mrs Pinchwife*. *Sir Jaspar Fidget* has been spelt throughout as he appears in the list of *Persons*, Jasp*ar*. The stage direction *Aside* has in every case been placed before the speech to which it refers.

ABBREVIATIONS

ed.	editor
O	octavo of 1713
O.E.D.	*Oxford English Dictionary*
PQ	Philological Quarterly
s.d.	stage direction
s.p.	speech prefix
Q1	first quarto 1675
Q2	edition of 1683
Q3	edition of 1688
Q4	edition of 1695
Q5	second edition of 1695

FURTHER READING

Horace Walpole, 'Thoughts on Comedy' (1798), available *Essays in Criticism*, XV (1965), 162–70.

William Hazlitt, *Lectures on the English Comic Writers* (1819).

Thomas Babington Macaulay, 'The Dramatic Works of Wycherley, Congreve, Vanbrugh & Farquhar', *Edinburgh Review*, LXXII (1841), 490–528.

Charles Perromat, *William Wycherley. Sa Vie—Son Oeuvre* (Paris, 1921).

Bonamy Dobrée, *Restoration Comedy 1660–1720* (Oxford, 1924).

Thomas H. Fujimura, *The Restoration Comedy of Wit* (Princeton, 1952).

Norman N. Holland, *The First Modern Comedies* (Cambridge, Mass., 1959).

Rose A. Zimbardo, *Wycherley's Drama. A link in the development of English satire* (New Haven and London, 1965).

Anne Righter, 'William Wycherley', available both in *Restoration Theatre (Stratford-Upon-Avon Studies* 6), ed. John Russell Brown and Bernard Harris (1965) and *Restoration Dramatists*, ed. Earl Miner (Englewood Cliffs, N.J., 1966).

Ronald Berman, 'The Ethic of *The Country Wife*', *Texas Studies in Literature and Language*, IX (1967), 47–55.

John Barnard, 'Drama from the Restoration till 1710', *English Drama to 1710* (Sphere History of Literature in the English Language 3), ed. C. Ricks (1971).

THE

Country-Wife,

A

COMEDY,

Acted at the

THEATRE ROYAL.

Written by Mr. *Wycherley.*

*Indignor quicquam reprehendi, non quia crasse
Compositum illepidéve putetur, sed quia nuper:
Nec veniam. Antiquis, sed honorem & præmia posci.*

Horat.

L O N D O N,

Printed for *Thomas Dring*, at the *Harrow*, at the
Corner of *Chancery-Lane* in *Fleet-street.* 1675..

Motto Horace, *Epistles*, II. i, 76–8: 'I am impatient that any work is censured, not because it is thought to be coarse or inelegant in style, but because it is modern, and that what is claimed for the ancients should be, not indulgence, but honour and rewards'. Wycherley may be suggesting that *The Country Wife* deserved praise for its crucial use, for Horner's disability, of the device from Terence's *Eunuchus* (*The Eunuch*), a play occasionally cited in Dryden's *Of Dramatick Poesie* (1668) during the debate between ancient and modern; Dryden gives part of the same Horatian epigraph to one of his characters, Eugenius, who defends the moderns.

PROLOGUE
Spoken by Mr Hart

Poets, like cudgelled bullies, never do
At first or second blow submit to you;
But will provoke you still and ne'er have done,
Till you are weary first with laying on.
The late so baffled scribbler of this day,   5
Though he stands trembling, bids me boldly say,
What we before most plays are used to do,
For poets out of fear first draw on you;
In a fierce prologue the still pit defy,
And, ere you speak, like Castril give the lie.   10
But though our Bayes's battles oft I've fought,
And with bruised knuckles their dear conquests bought;
Nay, never yet feared odds upon the stage,
In prologue dare not hector with the age,
But would take quarter from your saving hands,   15
Though Bayes within all yielding countermands,
Says you confederate wits no quarter give,
Therefore his play shalln't ask your leave to live.
Well, let the vain rash fop, by huffing so,
Think to obtain the better terms of you;   20
But we, the actors, humbly will submit,
Now, and at any time, to a full pit;
Nay, often we anticipate your rage,
And murder poets for you on our stage.

---

1 *bullies* ruffians of the London streets. The imagery of these metropolitan
  street hazards is maintained throughout the Prologue.
10 *Castril* the 'angry boy' in Ben Jonson's *The Alchemist*. The reference is
  to an exchange between Kastril and Subtle in IV. ii, 18 ff.
11 *Bayes* poet
16 *within* in the wings
19 *huffing* hectoring, blustering

---

5 *late so baffled scribbler* Wycherley, whose *The Gentleman Dancing
  Master* lasted only six days in 1672; 'being liked but indifferently, it was
  laid by to make room for other new ones', according to John Downes,
  Roscius Anglicanus (1708), p. 32
11 *Bayes* used to refer to Dryden in George Villiers's *The Rehearsal* (1671);
  here presumably an allusion to the fact that the speaker, Charles Hart,
  had played several heroes in Dryden tragedies

We set no guards upon our tiring-room,　　　　　　25
But when with flying colours there you come,
We patiently, you see, give up to you
Our poets, virgins, nay, our matrons too.

25 *tiring-room* dressing-room

THE PERSONS

MR HORNER	*Mr Hart*
MR HARCOURT	*Mr Kynaston*
MR DORILANT	*Mr Lydall*
MR PINCHWIFE	*Mr Mohun*
MR SPARKISH	*Mr Haines*
SIR JASPAR FIDGET	*Mr Cartwright*
MRS MARGERY PINCHWIFE	*Mrs Boutell*
MRS ALITHEA	*Mrs James*
MY LADY FIDGET	*Mrs Knepp*
MRS DAINTY FIDGET	*Mrs Corbet*
MRS SQUEAMISH	*Mrs Wyatt*
OLD LADY SQUEAMISH	*Mrs Rutter*
WAITERS, SERVANTS, AND ATTENDANTS	
A BOY	
A QUACK	*Mr Shatterell*
LUCY, *Alithea's Maid*	*Mrs Corey*

The Scene: *London*

5

THE COUNTRY WIFE

Act I, Scene i

Enter HORNER, *and* QUACK *following him at a distance*

HORNER (*Aside*)

A quack is as fit for a pimp as a midwife for a bawd; they are
still but in their way both helpers of nature.—Well, my dear
doctor, hast thou done what I desired?

QUACK

I have undone you for ever with the women, and reported
you throughout the whole town as bad as an eunuch, with as   5
much trouble as if I had made you one in earnest.

HORNER

But have you told all the midwives you know, the orange
wenches at the playhouses, the city husbands, and old
fumbling keepers of this end of the town? For they'll be the
readiest to report it!   10

QUACK

I have told all the chamber-maids, waiting-women, tire-
women and old women of my acquaintance; nay, and
whispered it as a secret to 'em, and to the whisperers of
Whitehall. So that you need not doubt 'twill spread, and you
will be as odious to the handsome young women as ...   15

HORNER

As the smallpox. Well ...

QUACK

And to the married women of this end of the town as ...

HORNER

As the great ones; nay, as their own husbands.

QUACK

And to the city dames as Aniseed Robin of filthy and contemptible memory; and they will frighten their children with   20
your name, especially their females.

9 *keepers* men who maintain a mistress
11 *all* (omit Q3)
11–12 *tire-women* ladies' maids
14 *Whitehall* the public rooms of the king's palace where gossip might be
   expected to flourish
18 *great ones* syphilis
19 *Aniseed Robin* a famous hermaphrodite and hero of various sexual
   escapades. Charles Cotton wrote an epitaph on him. *Poems* (1689)

HORNER

And cry, 'Horner's coming to carry you away!' I am only afraid 'twill not be believed. You told 'em 'twas by an English-French disaster, and an English-French chirurgeon, who has given me at once not only a cure but an antidote for 25 the future against that damned malady, and that worse distemper, love, and all other women's evils.

QUACK

Your late journey into France has made it the more credible, and your being here a fortnight before you appeared in public looks as if you apprehended the shame—which I wonder you 30 do not. Well, I have been hired by young gallants to belie 'em t'other way, but you are the first would be thought a man unfit for women.

HORNER

Dear Mr Doctor, let vain rogues be contented only to be thought abler men than they are, generally 'tis all the pleasure 35 they have; but mine lies another way.

QUACK

You take, methinks, a very preposterous way to it, and as ridiculous as if we operators in physic should put forth bills to disparage our medicaments, with hopes to gain customers. 40

HORNER

Doctor, there are quacks in love, as well as physic, who get but the fewer and worse patients for their boasting. A good name is seldom got by giving it oneself, and women no more than honour are compassed by bragging. Come, come, doctor, the wisest lawyer never discovers the merits of his 45 cause till the trial. The wealthiest man conceals his riches, and the cunning gamester his play. Shy husbands and keepers, like old rooks, are not to be cheated but by a new unpractised trick. False friendship will pass now no more than false dice upon 'em—no, not in the city. 50

Enter BOY

BOY

There are two ladies and a gentleman coming up.

[*Exit* BOY]

24 *English-French disaster* French pox was venereal disease, here perhaps caught of an English prostitute
24 *chirurgeon* surgeon
45 *discovers* reveals
48 *rooks* (rocks O) cheats: but see also I.i, 244
49 *pass* (omit O)

HORNER

A pox! Some unbelieving sisters of my former acquaintance
who, I am afraid, expect their sense should be satisfied of the
falsity of the report. No—this formal fool and women!

Enter SIR JASPAR, LADY FIDGET *and* MRS DAINTY FIDGET

QUACK

His wife and sister.   55

SIR JASPAR

My coach breaking just now before your door, sir, I look
upon as an occasional reprimand to me, sir, for not kissing
your hands, sir, since your coming out of France, sir; and so
my disaster, sir, has been my good fortune, sir; and this is my
wife and sister, sir.   60

HORNER

What then, sir?

SIR JASPAR

My lady and sister, sir.—Wife, this is Master Horner.

LADY FIDGET

Master Horner, husband!

SIR JASPAR

My lady, my Lady Fidget, sir.

HORNER

So, sir.   65

SIR JASPAR

Won't you be acquainted with her, sir? (*Aside*) So, the report
is true, I find, by his coldness or aversion to the sex; but I'll
play the wag with him.—Pray salute my wife, my lady, sir.

HORNER

I will kiss no man's wife, sir, for him, sir; I have taken my
eternal leave, sir, of the sex already, sir.   70

SIR JASPAR (*Aside*)

Ha, ha, ha! I'll plague him yet.—Not know my wife, sir?

HORNER

I do know your wife, sir, she's a woman, sir, and consequently a monster, sir, a greater monster than a husband,
sir.

SIR JASPAR

A husband! How, sir?   75

HORNER (*Makes horns*)

So, sir. But I make no more cuckolds, sir.

54 *formal* unmistakable, complete
57 *occasional* timely
76 s.d. (*Makes horns*) sign of a cuckold

SIR JASPAR
Ha, ha, ha! Mercury, Mercury!

LADY FIDGET
Pray, Sir Jaspar, let us be gone from this rude fellow.

DAINTY
Who, by his breeding, would think he had ever been in
France?   80

LADY FIDGET
Foh! he's but too much a French fellow, such as hate
women of quality and virtue for their love to their husbands,
Sir Jaspar. A woman is hated by 'em as much for loving her
husband as for loving their money. But pray let's be gone.

HORNER
You do well, madam, for I have nothing that you came for. I   85
have brought over not so much as a bawdy picture, new
postures, nor the second part of the *Ecole des Filles*, nor. . . .

QUACK (*Apart to* HORNER)
Hold for shame, sir! What d'ye mean? You'll ruin yourself
for ever with the sex. . . .

SIR JASPAR   90
Ha, ha, ha! He hates women perfectly, I find.

DAINTY
What pity 'tis he should.

LADY FIDGET
Ay, he's a base rude fellow for't; but affectation makes not a
woman more odious to them than virtue.

HORNER
Because your virtue is your greatest affectation, madam.

LADY FIDGET
How, you saucy fellow! Would you wrong my honour?   95

77 *Mercury* used to treat venereal disease. Perhaps also a covert allusion to
Mercury as the god, among other things, of traders and thieves

86–7 *new postures* indecent engravings to illustrate such erotic poems as
Pietro Aretino's *Sonnetti lussuriosi*
87 *Ecole des Filles* was issued but suppressed in Paris in 1655, being reissued
at various later dates and appearing last in England in 1744. According
to Pepys (13 January 1668) it was 'the most bawdy, lewd book that ever
I saw'; nonetheless he bought it. The similarly curious may consult it in
a cheap modern paperback: Michael Millot and Jean l'Ange, *The
School of Venus: or, the Ladies Delight reduced into rules of practice*—
which was its contemporary title in the English versions—translated
with an introduction by Donald Thomas (London, 1972). Perhaps the
only real point of contact it has with Wycherley's play is its discussion
of the mode of kissing that Margery tells her husband was employed by
Horner when he takes her into a house by the Exchange (IV,ii, 35)

HORNER

If I could.

LADY FIDGET

How d'you mean, sir?

SIR JASPAR

Ha, ha, ha! No, he can't wrong your ladyship's honour, upon
my honour! He, poor man—hark you in your ear—a mere
eunuch.   100

LADY FIDGET

O filthy French beast! foh, foh! Why do we stay? Let's be
gone. I can't endure the sight of him.

SIR JASPAR

Stay but till the chairs come. They'll be here presently.

LADY FIDGET

No, no.

SIR JASPAR

Nor can I stay longer. 'Tis—let me see—a quarter and a half   105
quarter of a minute past eleven. The Council will be sat, I
must away. Business must be preferred always before love
and ceremony with the wise, Mr Horner.

HORNER

And the impotent, Sir Jaspar.

SIR JASPAR

Ay, ay, the impotent, Master Horner, ha, ha, ha!   110

LADY FIDGET

What, leave us with a filthy man alone in his lodgings?

SIR JASPAR

He's an innocent man now, you know. Pray stay, I'll hasten
the chairs to you. Mr Horner, your servant; I should be glad
to see you at my house. Pray come and dine with me, and
play at cards with my wife after dinner—you are fit for   115
women at that game yet, ha, ha! (*Aside*) 'Tis as much a
husband's prudence to provide innocent diversion for a wife
as to hinder her unlawful pleasures, and he had better
employ her than let her employ herself.—Farewell.

Exit SIR JASPAR

HORNER

Your servant, Sir Jaspar.   120

LADY FIDGET

I will not stay with him, foh!

HORNER

Nay, madam, I beseech you stay, if it be but to see I can be as
civil to ladies yet as they would desire.

103 *chairs* sedan chairs
     presently at once

LADY FIDGET

No, no, foh! You cannot be civil to ladies.

DAINTY

You as civil as ladies would desire!   125

LADY FIDGET

No, no, no! foh, foh, foh!

Exeunt LADY FIDGET *and* DAINTY

QUACK

Now I think, I, or you yourself, rather, have done your
business with the women.

HORNER

Thou art an ass. Don't you see already, upon the report and
my carriage, this grave man of business leaves his wife in my   130
lodgings, invites me to his house and wife, who before would
not be acquainted with me out of jealousy?

QUACK

Nay, by this means you may be the more acquainted with the
husbands, but the less with the wives.

HORNER

Let me alone; if I can but abuse the husbands, I'll soon   135
disabuse the wives! Stay—I'll reckon you up the advantages
I am like to have by my stratagem. First, I shall be rid of all
my old acquaintances, the most insatiable sorts of duns, that
invade our lodgings in a morning. And next to the pleasure of
making a new mistress is that of being rid of an old one, and   140
of all old debts; love, when it comes to be so, is paid the most
unwillingly.

QUACK

Well, you may be so rid of your old acquaintances, but how
will you get any new ones?

HORNER

Doctor, thou wilt never make a good chemist, thou art so   145
incredulous and impatient. Ask but all the young fellows of
the town, if they do not lose more time, like huntsmen, in
starting the game, than in running it down. One knows not
where to find 'em who will, or will not. Women of quality are
so civil you can hardly distinguish love from good breeding,   150
and a man is often mistaken. But now I can be sure she that
shows an aversion to me loves the sport—as those women
that are gone, whom I warrant to be right. And then the next

130 *carriage* conduct, behaviour. See above, p. xvii
138 *sorts* (sort Q5)
     duns importunate creditor or, maybe, dunce
145 *chemist* alchemist seeking the philosopher's stone
153 *right* i.e., apt for his sexual purposes

thing is, your women of honour, as you call 'em, are only
chary of their reputations, not their persons, and 'tis scandal   155
they would avoid, not men. Now may I have, by the reputation of an eunuch, the privileges of one; and be seen in a
lady's chamber in a morning as early as her husband; kiss
virgins before their parents or lovers; and may be, in short,
the *passe partout* of the town. Now doctor. . . .   160

QUACK

Nay, now you shall be the doctor. And your process is so
new that we do not know but it may succeed.

HORNER

Not so new neither. *Probatum est*, doctor.

QUACK

Well, I wish you luck and many patients whilst I go to mine.
Exit QUACK

Enter HARCOURT *and* DORILANT *to* HORNER

HARCOURT

Come, your appearance at the play yesterday has, I hope,   165
hardened you for the future against the women's contempt
and the men's raillery, and now you'll abroad as you were
wont.

HORNER

Did I not bear it bravely?

DORILANT

With a most theatrical impudence! Nay, more than the   170
orange-wenches show there, or a drunken vizard-mask, or a
great-bellied actress. Nay, or the most impudent of
creatures—an ill poet. Or, what is yet more impudent, a
second-hand critic.

HORNER

But what say the ladies? Have they no pity?   175

HARCOURT

What ladies? The vizard-masks, you know, never pity a man
when all's gone, though in their service.

DORILANT

And for the women in the boxes, you'd never pity them when
'twas in your power.

160 *passe partout* leave or permit to go anywhere
163 *Probatum est* it has been proved or tested; phrase used on prescriptions
171 *vizard-mask* prostitute, so called from the masks they customarily wore
178 *women* (woman Q5)

163 *Probatum est* though Horner is probably saying that in the sex game
nothing, even his device, is new, Wycherley may also be hinting at his
revival of Terence's stratagem that had been invoked also by Jonson in
Act V of *Epicoene, or the Silent Woman*

HARCOURT
  They say—'tis pity, but all that deal with common women   180
  should be served so.

DORILANT
  Nay, I dare swear, they won't admit you to play at cards with
  them, go to plays with 'em, or do the little duties which other
  shadows of men are wont to do for 'em.

HORNER
  Who do you call shadows of men?   185

DORILANT
  Half-men.

HORNER
  What, boys?

DORILANT
  Ay, your old boys, old *beaux garçons*, who like superannuated
  stallions are suffered to run, feed, and whinny with the mares
  as long as they live, though they can do nothing else.   190

HORNER
  Well, a pox on love and wenching! Women serve but to keep
  a man from better company. Though I can't enjoy them I
  shall you the more. Good fellowship and friendship are
  lasting, rational, and manly pleasures.

HARCOURT
  For all that, give me some of those pleasures you call   195
  effeminate too. They help to relish one another.

HORNER
  They disturb one another.

HARCOURT
  No, mistresses are like books—if you pore upon them too
  much they doze you and make you unfit for company, but if
  used discreetly you are the fitter for conversation by 'em. 200

DORILANT
  A mistress should be like a little country retreat near the
  town—not to dwell in constantly, but only for a night and
  away, to taste the town the better when a man returns.

HORNER
  I tell you, 'tis as hard to be a good fellow, a good friend, and
  a lover of women, as 'tis to be a good fellow, a good friend, 205
  and a lover of money. You cannot follow both, then choose
  your side. Wine gives you liberty, love takes it away.

DORILANT
  Gad, he's in the right on't.

188 *beaux garçons* retired rakes acting as cicisbeos or gigolos
199 *doze* befuddle, confuse

HORNER

Wine gives you joy; love, grief and tortures, besides the
chirurgeon's. Wine makes us witty; love, only sots. Wine   210
makes us sleep; love breaks it.

DORILANT

By the world, he has reason, Harcourt.

HORNER

Wine makes . . .

DORILANT

Ay wine makes us . . . makes us princes; love makes us
beggars, poor rogues, i'gad . . . and wine . . .   215

HORNER

So, there's one converted. No, no, love and wine—oil and
vinegar.

HARCOURT

I grant it; love will still be uppermost.

HORNER

Come, for my part I will have only those glorious, manly
pleasures of being drunk and very slovenly.   220

Enter BOY

BOY

Mr Sparkish is below, sir.

[*Exit* BOY]

HARCOURT

What, my dear friend! A rogue that is fond of me only, I
think, for abusing him.

DORILANT

No, he can no more think the men laugh at him than that
women jilt him, his opinion of himself is so good.   225

HORNER

Well, there's another pleasure by drinking I thought not of—
I shall lose his acquaintance, because he cannot drink. And
you know 'tis a very hard thing to be rid of him for he's one
of those nauseous offerers at wit, who, like the worst fiddlers,
run themselves into all companies.   230

HARCOURT

One that by being in the company of men of sense would
pass for one.

---

210 *chirurgeon's. Wine* (chirurgeon's wine Q1–5, 0) I have here followed the
    reading of *Plays*, 2 vols. (1720)
213 *makes* (Makes us Q3)
214 *wine makes us* (wine makes Q5)
229 *offerers* those who attempt or offer

HORNER

And may so to the short-sighted world, as a false jewel
amongst true ones is not discerned at a distance. His company is as troublesome to us as a cuckold's when you have a   235
mind to his wife's.

HARCOURT

No, the rogue will not let us enjoy one another, but ravishes
our conversation, though he signifies no more to't than Sir
Martin Mar-all's gaping and awkward thrumming upon the
lute does to his man's voice and music.   240

DORILANT

And to pass for a wit in town shows himself a fool every night
to us, that are guilty of the plot.

HORNER

Such wits as he are, to a company of reasonable men, like
rooks to the gamesters, who only fill a room at the table, but
are so far from contributing to the play that they only serve to   245
spoil the fancy of those that do.

DORILANT

Nay, they are used like rooks too, snubbed, checked, and
abused; yet the rogues will hang on.

HORNER

A pox upon 'em, and all that force nature, and would be still
what she forbids 'em! Affectation is her greatest monster.   250

HARCOURT

Most men are the contraries to that they would seem. Your
bully, you see, is a coward with a long sword; the little,
humbly fawning physician with his ebony cane is he that
destroys men.

DORILANT

The usurer, a poor rogue possessed of mouldy bonds and   255
mortgages; and we they call spendthrifts are only wealthy,
who lay out his money upon daily new purchases of
pleasure.

233   *to* (omit Q5)
233   *short-sighted* Q2–5, 0 (short-sighed Q1)
244   *rooks* gulls. *OED* allows the word to mean those who cheat (see I.i, 48)
        and, as here, those who are cheated

238–9   *Sir Martin Mar-all's gaping* the eponymous hero of Dryden's comedy
        of 1667 who serenades his mistress by pretending to sing and play upon
        his lute, while in effect his servant is performing just out of sight. The
        deception is discovered by Sir Martin's neglecting to stop at the right
        time

HORNER

Ay, your arrantest cheat is your trustee, or executor; your
jealous man, the greatest cuckold; your churchman, the 260
greatest atheist; and your noisy, pert rogue of a wit, the
greatest fop, dullest ass, and worst company, as you shall see
—for here he comes.

Enter SPARKISH *to them*

SPARKISH

How is't, sparks, how is't? Well, faith, Harry, I must rally
thee a little, ha, ha, ha! upon the report in town of thee, ha, 265
ha, ha! I can't hold i'faith—shall I speak?

HORNER

Yes, but you'll be so bitter then.

SPARKISH.

Honest Dick and Frank here shall answer for me, I will not
be extreme bitter, by the universe.

HARCOURT

We will be bound in ten thousand pound bond, he shall not 270
be bitter at all.

DORILANT

Nor sharp, nor sweet.

HORNER

What, not downright insipid?

SPARKISH

Nay then, since you are so brisk and provoke me, take what
follows. You must know, I was discoursing and rallying with 275
some ladies yesterday, and they happened to talk of the fine
new signs in town.

HORNER

Very fine ladies, I believe.

SPARKISH

Said I, 'I know where the best new sign is'. 'Where?' says
one of the ladies. 'In Covent Garden', I replied. Said another, 280
'In what street?' 'In Russell Street', answered I. 'Lord', says
another, 'I'm sure there was ne'er a fine new sign there
yesterday'. 'Yes, but there was', said I again, 'and it came
out of France, and has been there a fortnight'.

264 *rally* pull together, revive, rouse
277 *signs* tradesmen's boards

---

280 *Covent Garden* fashionable area north of the Strand, with several
   famous taverns and coffee-houses; originally the Convent Garden of
   the monks of Westminster, it was transformed into a square in 1640 by
   Inigo Jones
281 *Russell Street* off east side of Covent Garden

DORILANT

A pox! I can hear no more, prithee.   285

HORNER

No, hear him out; let him tune his crowd a while.

HARCOURT

The worst music, the greatest preparation.

SPARKISH

Nay, faith, I'll make you laugh. 'It cannot be', says a third
lady. 'Yes, yes', quoth I again. Says a fourth lady. . . .

HORNER

Look to't, we'll have no more ladies.   290

SPARKISH

No . . . then mark, mark, now. Said I to the fourth, 'Did you
never see Mr Horner? He lodges in Russell Street, and he's a
sign of a man, you know, since he came out of France!'.He,
ha, he!

HORNER

But the devil take me, if thine be the sign of a jest.   295

SPARKISH

With that they all fell a-laughing, till they bepissed themselves. What, but it does not move you, methinks? Well, I
see one has as good go to law without a witness, as break a
jest without a laugher on one's side. Come, come sparks, but
where do we dine? I have left at Whitehall an earl to dine   300
with you.

DORILANT

Why, I thought thou hadst loved a man with a title better
than a suit with a French trimming to't.

HARCOURT

Go to him again.

SPARKISH

No, sir, a wit to me is the greatest title in the world.   305

HORNER

But go dine with your earl, sir; he may be exceptious. We are
your friends, and will not take it ill to be left, I do assure you.

HARCOURT

Nay, faith, he shall go to him.

286 *crowd* fiddle. But also perhaps a joke among those who know him about
    Sparkish's tales of himself entertaining crowds of listeners: see I.i,
    289–90
297 *I* Q3, 0 (omit Q1–2, Q4–5)
299 *laugher* Q1 (laughter Q2–5, 0) i.e., a joke needs someone to laugh at it
    as a law-suit needs a witness on its side
303 *suit with a French trimming* perhaps a reference to Horner's 'state'
306 *exceptious* peevish, vexed

SPARKISH

Nay, pray, gentlemen.

DORILANT

We'll thrust you out, if you won't. What, disappoint   310
anybody for us?

SPARKISH

Nay, dear gentlemen, hear me.

HORNER

No, no, sir, by no means; pray go, sir.

SPARKISH

Why, dear rogues . . .

DORILANT

No, no.   315

They all thrust him out of the room

ALL

Ha, ha, ha!

SPARKISH *returns*

SPARKISH

But, sparks, pray hear me. What, d'ye think I'll eat, then, with
gay shallow fops and silent coxcombs? I think wit as
necessary at dinner as a glass of good wine, and that's the
reason I never have any stomach when I eat alone. Come, but   320
where do we dine?

HORNER

Even where you will.

SPARKISH

At Chateline's?

DORILANT

Yes, if you will.

SPARKISH

Or at the Cock?   325

DORILANT

Yes, if you please.

SPARKISH

Or at the Dog and Partridge?

323–7 *Chateline's . . . Cock . . . Dog and Partridge* Chatelin's was a French
restaurant or 'ordinary' in Covent Garden; the Dog and Partridge, one in
Fleet Street. The Cock—and there were many Cocks—was possibly
the tavern in Bow Street, Covent Garden, where Wycherley set part of
Act V of *The Plain Dealer*, and where Wycherley's wife, the Countess of
Drogheda, allowed him visits, provided that the windows were left
open so that she could see from their lodgings opposite that there were
no females among the company

HORNER

Ay, if you have a mind to't, for we shall dine at neither.

SPARKISH

Pshaw! with your fooling we shall lose the new play. And I
would no more miss seeing a new play the first day than I   330
would miss setting in the wits' row. Therefore I'll go fetch
my mistress and away.

Exit SPARKISH

Manent HORNER, HARCOURT, DORILANT, *Enter to them* MR PINCHWIFE

HORNER

Who have we here? Pinchwife?

PINCHWIFE

Gentlemen, your humble servant.

HORNER

Well, Jack, by thy long absence from the town, the grumness   335
of thy countenance, and the slovenliness of thy habit, I should
give thee joy, should I not, of marriage?

PINCHWIFE (*Aside*)

Death! does he know I'm married too? I thought to have
concealed it from him at least.—My long stay in the country
will excuse my dress, and I have a suit of law, that brings me   340
up to town, that puts me out of humour. Besides, I must give
Sparkish tomorrow five thousand pound to lie with my sister.

HORNER

Nay, you country gentlemen, rather than not purchase, will
buy anything; and he is a cracked title, if we may quibble.
Well, but am I to give thee joy? I heard thou wert married.   345

PINCHWIFE

What then?

HORNER

Why, the next thing that is to be heard is, thou'rt a cuckold.

PINCHWIFE (*Aside*)

Insupportable name!

HORNER

But I did not expect marriage from such a whoremaster as
you, one that knew the town so much, and women so well.   350

---

328 *a mind* (mind Q1)
331 *setting* (sitting Q3)
335 *grumness* moroseness
342 *five thousand pound* as dowry
344 *cracked title* unsound claim to ownership and so—*à propos* Sparkish—
presumably a bad buy as a brother-in-law
349 *whoremaster* fornicator

PINCHWIFE

Why, I have married no London wife.

HORNER

Pshaw! that's all one. That grave circumspection in marrying
a country wife is like refusing a deceitful, pampered Smithfield jade to go and be cheated by a friend in the country.

PINCHWIFE (*Aside*)

A pox on him and his simile!—At least we are a little surer   355
of the breed there, know what her keeping has been, whether
foiled or unsound.

HORNER

Come, come, I have known a clap gotten in Wales. And
there are cozens, justices, clerks, and chaplains in the
country—I won't say coachmen! But she's handsome and   360
young?

PINCHWIFE (*Aside*)

I'll answer as I should do.—No, no, she has no beauty but
her youth; no attraction but her modesty; wholesome,
homely, and housewifely, that's all.

DORILANT

He talks as like a grazier as he looks.   365

PINCHWIFE

She's too awkward, ill-favoured, and silly to bring to town.

HARCOURT

Then methinks you should bring her, to be taught breeding.

PINCHWIFE

To be taught! No, sir, I thank you. Good wives and private
soldiers should be ignorant. [*Aside*] I'll keep her from your
instructions, I warrant you.   370

355 *a* Q1 (omit Q2–5, 0)
357 *foiled* injured, defective (horse); deflowered or diseased (woman)
358 *clap* venereal disease
359 *cozens* cheaters, those who cozen. Unnecessarily emended by some
      editors to *cousins*, which has no relevant meaning here
359 *justices, clerks* (justices clerks Q5) Horner is making a fairly cynical list
      so that it is worth allowing the reading that adds two 'respectables' to
      those purveying VD in the provinces
365 *grazier* grazer of cattle fattened for market: so it is their salesman talk
      that is referred to here
366 *silly* ignorant

353–4 *Smithfield jade* Smithfield horse market had a reputation for sharp
      dealing and since *jade* means a disreputable woman as well as a worn-out
      horse the comparison Horner makes is apt
367 *breeding* one suspects, among those mocking Pinchwife, that this might
      be intended—or at least received—as an indecency

HARCOURT (*Aside*)
  The rogue is as jealous as if his wife were not ignorant.
HORNER
  Why, if she be ill-favoured, there will be less danger here for
  you than by leaving her in the country. We have such variety
  of dainties that we are seldom hungry.
DORILANT
  But they always have coarse, constant, swinging stomachs   375
  in the country.
HARCOURT
  Foul feeders indeed.
DORILANT
  And your hospitality is great there.
HARCOURT
  Open house, every man's welcome!
PINCHWIFE
  So, so, gentlemen.   380
HORNER
  But, prithee, why would'st thou marry her? If she be ugly,
  ill-bred, and silly, she must be rich then?
PINCHWIFE
  As rich as if she brought me twenty thousand pound out of
  this town; for she'll be as sure not to spend her moderate
  portion as a London baggage would be to spend hers, let it   385
  be what it would; so 'tis all one. Then, because she's ugly,
  she's the likelier to be my own; and being ill-bred, she'll hate
  conversation; and since silly and innocent, will not know the
  difference betwixt a man of one-and-twenty and one of
  forty.   390
HORNER
  Nine—to my knowledge; but if she be silly, she'll expect as
  much from a man of forty-nine as from him of one-and-
  twenty. But methinks wit is more necessary than beauty;
  and I think no young woman ugly that has it, and no handsome woman agreeable without it.   395
PINCHWIFE
  'Tis my maxim he's a fool that marries, but he's a greater
  that does not marry a fool. What is wit in a wife good for, but
  to make a man a cuckold?
HORNER
  Yes, to keep it from his knowledge.
PINCHWIFE
  A fool cannot contrive to make her husband a cuckold.   400

375 *swinging stomachs* huge appetites

HORNER

No, but she'll club with a man that can; and what is worse, if
she cannot make her husband a cuckold, she'll make him
jealous, and pass for one, and then 'tis all one.

PINCHWIFE

Well, well, I'll take care for one, my wife shall make me no
cuckold, though she had your help, Mr Horner; I under-   405
stand the town, sir.

DORILANT (*Aside*)

His help!

HARCOURT (*Aside*)

He's come newly to town, it seems, and has not heard how
things are with him.

HORNER

But tell me, has marriage cured thee of whoring, which it   410
seldom does?

HARCOURT

'Tis more than age can do.

HORNER

No, the word is, I'll marry and live honest. But a marriage
vow is like a penitent gamester's oath, and entering into
bonds and penalties to stint himself to such a particular small   415
sum at play for the future, which makes him but the more
eager, and not being able to hold out, loses his money again,
and his forfeit to boot.

DORILANT

Ay, ay, a gamester will be a gamester whilst his money lasts,
and a whoremaster, whilst his vigour.   420

HARCOURT

Nay, I have known 'em, when they are broke and can lose no
more a-fumbling with the box in their hands to fool with
only, and hinder other gamesters.

DORILANT

That had wherewithal to make lusty stakes.

PINCHWIFE

Well, gentlemen, you may laugh at me, but you shall never   425
lie with my wife; I know the town.

---

401 *club* get together with
413 *honest* chaste

422–4 *fumbling with the box* . . . *lusty stakes* an undertow of indecency per-
    haps here that continues Dorilant's analogy between a gamester and a
    whoremaster. See Rochester's 'The Disabled Debauchee', for another
    Restoration variation on the theme of aged rakes

HORNER

But prithee, was not the way you were in better? Is not
keeping better than marriage?

PINCHWIFE

A pox on't! The jades would jilt me; I could never keep a
whore to myself.   430

HORNER

So, then, you only married to keep a whore to yourself. Well,
but let me tell you, women, as you say, are like soldiers, made
constant and loyal by good pay rather than by oaths and
covenants. Therefore I'd advise my friends to keep rather
than marry, since too I find, by your example, it does not   435
serve one's turn—for I saw you yesterday in the eighteen-
penny place with a pretty country wench!

PINCHWIFE (*Aside*)

How the devil! Did he see my wife then? I sat there that she
might not be seen. But she shall never go to a play again.

HORNER

What, dost thou blush at nine-and-forty for having been   **440**
seen with a wench?

DORILANT

No, faith, I warrant 'twas his wife, which he seated there out
of sight, for he's a cunning rogue, and understands the town.

HARCOURT

He blushes! Then 'twas his wife—for men are now more
ashamed to be seen with them in public than with a wench.   445

PINCHWIFE (*Aside*)

Hell and damnation! I'm undone, since Horner has seen her,
and they know 'twas she.

HORNER

But prithee, was it thy wife? She was exceedingly pretty; I
was in love with her at that distance.

PINCHWIFE

You are like never to be nearer to her. Your servant,   450
gentlemen.

                                               Offers to go

HORNER

Nay, prithee stay.

428 *keeping* supporting a mistress
451 s.d. *Offers* attempts

436–7 *eighteen-penny place* middle gallery in theatre, frequented by the
    whores or *vizard masks*, and so a suitable enough place for Pinchwife to
    seat his wife so as not to let her be seen by the gallants in the pit or
    boxes below

PINCHWIFE
 I cannot, I will not.
HORNER
 Come, you shall dine with us.
PINCHWIFE
 I have dined already.   455
HORNER
 Come, I know thou hast not. I'll treat thee, dear rogue.
 Thou shan't spend none of thy Hampshire money today.
PINCHWIFE *(Aside)*
 Treat me! So, he uses me already like his cuckold!
HORNER
 Nay, you shall not go.
PINCHWIFE
 I must, I have business at home.   *Exit* PINCHWIFE   460
HARCOURT
 To beat his wife! He's as jealous of her as a Cheapside
 husband of a Covent Garden wife.
HORNER
 Why, 'tis as hard to find an old whoremaster without
 jealousy and the gout, as a young one without fear or the
 pox.   465
  As gout in age from pox in youth proceeds,
  So wenching past, then jealousy succeeds—
  The worst disease that love and wenching breeds.

Act II, Scene i

MRS MARGERY PINCHWIFE *and* ALITHEA; MR PINCHWIFE *peeping
behind at the door*

MRS PINCHWIFE
 Pray, sister, where are the best fields and woods to walk in,
 in London?
ALITHEA
 A pretty question! Why, sister, Mulberry Garden and St
 James's Park; and for close walks, the New Exchange.

461–2 *Cheapside husband* city merchant husband
462 *Covent Garden wife* fashionable, high-class wife
 4 *close* covered

 3–4 *Mulberry Garden and St James's Park . . . the New Exchange* popular
  gathering places, the second of which gives its name to the sub-title of
  Wycherley's *Love in a Wood*. All were, of course, formal designs and presumably not the country-like walks Margery seeks. Mulberry Garden,
  which gave its name to the play by Sedley of 1668, was called after a plan-

MRS PINCHWIFE

Pray, sister, tell me why my husband looks so grum here in   5
town, and keeps me up so close, and will not let me go
a-walking, nor let me wear my best gown yesterday?

ALITHEA

Oh, he's jealous, sister.

MRS PINCHWIFE

Jealous? What's that?

ALITHEA

He's afraid you should love another man.   10

MRS PINCHWIFE

How should he be afraid of my loving another man, when he
will not let me see any but himself.

ALITHEA

Did he not carry you yesterday to a play?

MRS PINCHWIFE

Ay, but we sat amongst ugly people. He would not let me
come near the gentry, who sat under us, so that I could not   15
see 'em. He told me none but naughty women sat there,
whom they toused and moused. But I would have ventured
for all that.

ALITHEA

But how did you like the play?

MRS PINCHWIFE

Indeed I was a-weary of the play, but I liked hugeously the   20
actors! They are the goodliest, properest men, sister.

ALITHEA

Oh, but you must not like the actors, sister.

MRS PINCHWIFE

Ay, how should I help it, sister? Pray, sister, when my
husband comes in, will you ask leave for me to go a-walking?

---

17 *toused and moused* rumpled and toyed with. *Mousled* is used with
similarly sexual force by Mrs Pinchwife in IV. ii, 36

20 *a-weary* Q1 (weary Q2–5, 0)

---

tation of mulberry trees ordered by James I and situated where Buckingham Palace now stands; Evelyn (10 May 1654) said it was the 'only place
of refreshment about the town for persons of quality to be exceedingly
cheated at'. Although a fashionable gathering place, St James's
Park had its seamier side, as witness Rochester's 'A Ramble in St
James's Park'. The New Exchange, an arcade with two long double
galleries of fashionable shops, was to the south of the Strand and was a
usual place for assignations—Mrs Pinchwife gets there in Act III.
Opened in 1609, the New Exchange was demolished in 1737.

ALITHEA (*Aside*)

A-walking! Ha, ha! Lord, a country gentlewoman's leisure is   25
the drudgery of a foot-post; and she requires as much airing
as her husband's horses.

Enter MR PINCHWIFE *to them*

But here comes your husband; I'll ask, though I'm sure he'll
not grant it.

MRS PINCHWIFE

He says he won't let me go abroad for fear of catching the   30
pox.

ALITHEA

Fie, the smallpox you should say.

MRS PINCHWIFE

Oh my dear, dear bud, welcome home! Why dost thou look
so fropish? Who has nangered thee?

PINCHWIFE

You're a fool!   35

                              MRS PINCHWIFE *goes aside and cries*

ALITHEA

Faith, so she is, for crying for no fault, poor tender creature!

PINCHWIFE

What, you would have her as impudent as yourself, as
arrant as a jill-flirt, a gadder, a magpie, and to say all—a
mere notorious town-woman?

ALITHEA

Brother, you are my only censurer; and the honour of your   40
family shall sooner suffer in your wife there than in me,
though I take the innocent liberty of the town.

PINCHWIFE

Hark you, mistress, do not talk so before my wife. The
innocent liberty of the town!

ALITHEA

Why, pray, who boasts of any intrigue with me? What   45
lampoon has made my name notorious? What ill women
frequent my lodgings? I keep no company with any women
of scandalous reputations.

25 *leisure* Q1 (pleasure Q2–5, 0)
26 *foot-post* letter-carrier on foot
33 *bud* honey bud, a double endearment
34 *fropish* peevish, fretful
    nangered angered
38 *jill-flirt* wanton girl
    magpie idle chatterer
46 *lampoon* virulent or scurrilous piece of satire

PINCHWIFE
 No, you keep the men of scandalous reputations company.
ALITHEA
 Where? Would you not have me civil? Answer 'em in a box   50
 at the plays, in the drawing room at Whitehall, in St James's
 Park, Mulberry Garden, or . . .
PINCHWIFE
 Hold, hold! Do not teach my wife where the men are to be
 found! I believe she's the worse for your town documents
 already. I bid you keep her in ignorance, as I do.   55
MRS PINCHWIFE
 Indeed, be not angry with her, bud. She will tell me nothing
 of the town though I ask her a thousand times a day.
PINCHWIFE
 Then you are very inquisitive to know, I find!
MRS PINCHWIFE
 Not I, indeed, dear. I hate London. Our placehouse in the
 country is worth a thousand of't. Would I were there again!   60
PINCHWIFE
 So you shall, I warrant. But were you not talking of plays and
 players when I came in? [*To* ALITHEA] You are her en-
 courager in such discourses.
MRS PINCHWIFE
 No, indeed, dear; she chid me just now for liking the player-
 men.   65
PINCHWIFE (*Aside*)
 Nay, if she be so innocent as to own to me her liking them,
 there is no hurt in't.—Come, my poor rogue, but thou lik'st
 none better than me?
MRS PINCHWIFE
 Yes, indeed, but I do; the player-men are finer folks.
PINCHWIFE
 But you love none better than me?   70
MRS PINCHWIFE
 You are mine own dear bud, and I know you; I hate a
 stranger.
PINCHWIFE
 Ay, my dear, you must love me only, and not be like the
 naughty town-women, who only hate their husbands and
 love every man else—love plays, visits, fine coaches, fine   75
 clothes, fiddles, balls, treats, and so lead a wicked town-life.

54 *town documents* provision of information about the town
59 *placehouse* chief house on an estate, that perhaps gives its name to the
   place
71 *mine* Q1 (my Q2–5, 0)

MRS PINCHWIFE

Nay, if to enjoy all these things be a town-life, London is not
so bad a place, dear.

PINCHWIFE

How! If you love me, you must hate London.

ALITHEA [*Aside*]

The fool has forbid me discovering to her the pleasures of the 80
town, and he is now setting her agog upon them himself.

MRS PINCHWIFE

But, husband, do the town-women love the player-men too?

PINCHWIFE

Yes, I warrant you.

MRS PINCHWIFE

Ay, I warrant you.

PINCHWIFE

Why, you do not, I hope? 85

MRS PINCHWIFE

No, no, bud; but why have we no player-men in the
country?

PINCHWIFE

Ha!—Mistress Minx, ask me no more to go to a play.

MRS PINCHWIFE

Nay, why love? I did not care for going, but when you forbid
me, you make me, as't were, desire it. 90

ALITHEA (*Aside*)

So 'twill be in other things, I warrant.

MRS PINCHWIFE

Pray, let me go to a play, dear.

PINCHWIFE

Hold your peace, I wo'not.

MRS PINCHWIFE

Why, love?

PINCHWIFE

Why, I'll tell you. 95

ALITHEA (*Aside*)

Nay, if he tell her, she'll give him more cause to forbid her
that place.

MRS PINCHWIFE

Pray, why, dear?

PINCHWIFE

First, you like the actors, and the gallants may like you.

MRS PINCHWIFE

What, a homely country girl? No, bud, nobody will like me. 100

90 *make me* Q1, Q3–4, 0 (make Q2, Q5)
93 *your* (you Q3)

PINCHWIFE

I tell you, yes, they may.

MRS PINCHWIFE

No, no, you jest—I won't believe you, I will go.

PINCHWIFE

I tell you then, that one of the lewdest fellows in town, who
saw you there, told me he was in love with you.

MRS PINCHWIFE

Indeed! Who, who, pray who was't?   105

PINCHWIFE (*Aside*)

I've gone too far, and slipped before I was aware. How
overjoyed she is!

MRS PINCHWIFE

Was it any Hampshire gallant, any of our neighbours? I
promise you, I am beholding to him.

PINCHWIFE

I promise you, you lie; for he would but ruin you, as he has 110
done hundreds. He has no other love for women, but that;
such as he look upon women, like basilisks, but to destroy
'em.

MRS PINCHWIFE

Ay, but if he loves me, why should he ruin me? Answer me
to that. Methinks he should not; I would do him no harm. 115

ALITHEA

Ha, ha, ha!

PINCHWIFE

'Tis very well; but I'll keep him from doing you any harm, or
me either.

Enter SPARKISH *and* HARCOURT

But here comes company; get you in, get you in.

MRS PINCHWIFE

But pray, husband; is he a pretty gentleman that loves me? 120

PINCHWIFE

 In, baggage, in!   (*Thrusts her in; shuts the door*)
[*Aside*] What, all the lewd libertines of the town brought to
my lodgings by this easy coxcomb! S'death, I'll not suffer it.

SPARKISH

Here Harcourt, do you approve my choice? [*To* ALITHEA]
Dear little rogue, I told you I'd bring you acquainted with 125
all my friends, the wits, and . . .

       HARCOURT *salutes her*

109 *beholding* grateful
112 *basilisks* legendary serpents whose glance was fatal

PINCHWIFE [*Aside*]

Ay, they shall know her, as well as you yourself will, I
warrant you.

SPARKISH

This is one of those, my pretty rogue, that are to dance at
your wedding tomorrow; and him you must bid welcome   130
ever to what you and I have.

PINCHWIFE (*Aside*)

Monstrous!

SPARKISH

Harcourt, how dost thou like her, faith?—Nay, dear, do not
look down; I should hate to have a wife of mine out of
countenance at any thing.   135

PINCHWIFE [*Aside*]

Wonderful!

SPARKISH

Tell me, I say, Harcourt, how dost thou like her? Thou hast
stared upon her enough to resolve me.

HARCOURT

So infinitely well that I could wish I had a mistress too, that
might differ from her in nothing but her love and engagement   140
to you.

ALITHEA

Sir, Master Sparkish has often told me that his acquaintance
were all wits and railleurs and now I find it.

SPARKISH

No, by the universe, madam, he does not rally now; you may
believe him. I do assure you, he is the honestest, worthiest,   145
true-hearted gentleman—a man of such perfect honour, he
would say nothing to a lady he does not mean.

PINCHWIFE (*Aside*)

Praising another man to his mistress!

HARCOURT

Sir, you are so beyond expectation obliging, that . . .

SPARKISH

Nay, i'gad, I am sure you do admire her extremely; I see't in   150
your eyes.—He does admire you, madam.—By the world,
don't you?

HARCOURT

Yes, above the world, or the most glorious part of it, her
whole sex; and till now I never thought I should have
envied you or any man about to marry, but you have the   155
best excuse for marriage I ever knew.

ALITHEA

Nay, now, sir, I'm satisfied you are of the society of the wits

and railleurs since you cannot spare your friend even when
he is but too civil to you. But the surest sign is, since you are
an enemy to marriage, for that, I hear, you hate as much as   160
business or bad wine.

HARCOURT

Truly, madam, I never was an enemy to marriage till now,
because marriage was never an enemy to me before.

ALITHEA

But why, sir, is marriage an enemy to you now? Because it
robs you of your friend here? For you look upon a friend   165
married as one gone into a monastery, that is dead to the
world.

HARCOURT

'Tis indeed, because you marry him; I see, madam, you can
guess my meaning. I do confess heartily and openly, I wish
it were in my power to break the match. By heavens I   170
would!

SPARKISH

Poor Frank.

ALITHEA

Would you be so unkind to me?

HARCOURT

No, no, 'tis not because I would be unkind to you.

SPARKISH

Poor Frank! No, gad, 'tis only his kindness to me.   175

PINCHWIFE (*Aside*)

Great kindness to you indeed! Insensible fop, let a man make
love to his wife to his face!

SPARKISH

Come, dear Frank, for all my wife there that shall be, thou
shalt enjoy me sometimes, dear rogue. By my honour, we
men of wit condole for our deceased brother in marriage as   180
much as for one dead in earnest.—I think that was prettily said
of me, ha, Harcourt?—But come, Frank, be not melancholy
for me.

HARCOURT

No, I assure you I am not melancholy for you.

SPARKISH

Prithee, Frank, dost think my wife that shall be, there, a fine   185
person?

HARCOURT

I could gaze upon her till I became as blind as you are.

158 *railleurs* banterers
162 *never was* (was never Q2–5, 0)
182 *not* (not not Q1)

SPARKISH
How, as I am? How?
HARCOURT
Because you are a lover, and true lovers are blind, stock
blind.   190
SPARKISH
True, true; but by the world, she has wit too, as well as
beauty. Go, go with her into a corner, and try if she has wit;
talk to her anything; she's bashful before me.
HARCOURT
Indeed, if a woman wants wit in a corner, she has it nowhere.
ALITHEA (*Aside to* SPARKISH)
Sir, you dispose of me a little before your time . . .   195
SPARKISH
Nay, nay, madam, let me have an earnest of your obedience
or . . . Go, go, madam. . . .

                              HARCOURT *courts* ALITHEA *aside*
PINCHWIFE
How, sir! If you are not concerned for the honour of a wife, I
am for that of a sister; he shall not debauch her. Be a pander
to your own wife, bring men to her, let 'em make love before   200
your face, thrust 'em into a corner together, then leave 'em in
private! Is this your town wit and conduct?
SPARKISH
Ha, ha, ha! A silly wise rogue would make one laugh more
than a stark fool, ha, ha! I shall burst. Nay, you shall not
disturb 'em; I'll vex thee, by the world. *Struggles with*   205
        PINCHWIFE *to keep him from* HARCOURT *and* ALITHEA
ALITHEA
The writings are drawn, sir, settlements made; 'tis too late,
sir, and past all revocation.
HARCOURT
Then so is my death.
ALITHEA
I would not be unjust to him.
HARCOURT
Then why to me so?   210
ALITHEA
I have no obligation to you.
HARCOURT
My love.

189–90 *stock blind* as blind as a lifeless thing. But since *stock* had also come to
    mean a stupid person, also perhaps double-edged as 'stupidly blind'
205 *vex* prevent, frustrate

ALITHEA

I had his before.

HARCOURT

You never had it; he wants, you see, jealousy, the only
infallible sign of it.   215

ALITHEA

Love proceeds from esteem; he cannot distrust my virtue.
Besides he loves me, or he would not marry me.

HARCOURT

Marrying you is no more sign of his love, than bribing your
woman, that he may marry you, is a sign of his generosity.
Marriage is rather a sign of interest than love; and he that   220
marries a fortune, covets a mistress, not loves her. But if you
take marriage for a sign of love, take it from me immediately.

ALITHEA

No, now you have put a scruple in my head. But in short, sir,
to end our dispute—I must marry him, my reputation would   225
suffer in the world else.

HARCOURT

No, if you do marry him, with your pardon, madam, your
reputation suffers in the world, and you would be thought in
necessity for a cloak.

ALITHEA

Nay, now you are rude, sir.—Mr Sparkish, pray come   230
hither, your friend here is very troublesome, and very loving.

HARCOURT (*Aside to* ALITHEA)

Hold, hold!

PINCHWIFE

D'ye hear that?

SPARKISH

Why, d'ye think I'll seem to be jealous, like a country
bumpkin?   235

PINCHWIFE

No, rather be a cuckold, like a credulous cit.

HARCOURT

Madam, you would not have been so little generous as to have
told him?

ALITHEA

Yes, since you could be so little generous as to wrong him.

220 *than* Q4–5, 0 (then Q1–3)
220 *love* (lover 0)
229 *necessity for a cloak* to hide pregnancy
236 *cit* disparaging word for citizen, differentiating him from gentry

HARCOURT
Wrong him! No man can do't, he's beneath an injury; a 240
bubble, a coward, a senseless idiot, a wretch so con-
temptible to all the world but you that . . .
ALITHEA
Hold, do not rail at him, for since he is like to be my husband
I am resolved to like him. Nay, I think I am obliged to tell
him you are not his friend.—Master Sparkish, Master 245
Sparkish!
SPARKISH
What, what? Now, dear rogue, has not she wit?
HARCOURT (*Speaks surlily*)
Not as much as I thought, and hoped she had.
ALITHEA
Mr Sparkish, do you bring people to rail at you?
HARCOURT
Madam . . .   250
SPARKISH
How! No, but if he does rail at me, 'tis but in jest, I warrant
—what we wits do for one another and never take any
notice of it.
ALITHEA
He spoke so scurrilously of you, I had no patience to hear
him; besides, he has been making love to me.   255
HARCOURT (*Aside*)
True, damned, tell-tale woman.
SPARKISH
Pshaw! to show his parts—we wits rail and make love often
but to show our parts; as we have no affections, so we have
no malice; we . . .
ALITHEA
He said you were a wretch, below an injury.   260
SPARKISH
Pshaw!
HARCOURT [*Aside*]
Damned, senseless, impudent, virtuous jade! Well, since she
won't let me have her, she'll do as good, she'll make me hate
her.
ALITHEA
A common bubble.   265
SPARKISH
Pshaw!
ALITHEA
A coward.

241 *bubble* fool (? easily deflated, like a bubble)

SPARKISH
Pshaw, pshaw!

ALITHEA
A senseless, drivelling idiot.

SPARKISH
How! Did he disparage my parts? Nay, then my honour's   270
concerned. I can't put up that, sir, by the world. Brother,
help me to kill him. (*Aside*) I may draw now, since we have
the odds of him! 'Tis a good occasion, too, before my
mistress. . . .

Offers to draw

ALITHEA
Hold, hold!   275

SPARKISH
What, what?

ALITHEA (*Aside*) ·
I must not let 'em kill the gentleman neither, for his kindness
to me; I am so far from hating him that I wish my gallant
had his person and understanding.—Nay, if my honour . . .

SPARKISH
I'll be thy death.   280

ALITHEA
Hold, hold! Indeed, to tell the truth, the gentleman said
after all that what he spoke was but out of friendship to you.

SPARKISH
How! say, I am—I am a fool, that is, no wit, out of friendship to me?

ALITHEA
Yes, to try whether I was concerned enough for you, and   285
made love to me only to be satisfied of my virtue, for your sake.

HARCOURT (*Aside*)
Kind however . . .

SPARKISH
Nay, if it were so, my dear rogue, I ask thee pardon. But why
would not you tell me so, faith?

HARCOURT
Because I did not think on't, faith.   290

SPARKISH
Come, Horner does not come. Harcourt, let's be gone to the
new play. Come, madam.

283 *wit* (whit Q5)
286 *made* (make Q5)
288 s.p. SPARKISH (omit 0)

ALITHEA

I will not go, if you intend to leave me alone in the box and
run into the pit, as you use to do.

SPARKISH

Pshaw! I'll leave Harcourt with you in the box to entertain   295
you and that's as good. If I sat in the box I should be thought
no judge but of trimmings.—Come away, Harcourt, lead her
down.

Exeunt SPARKISH, HARCOURT *and* ALITHEA

PINCHWIFE

Well, go thy ways, for the flower of the true town fops, such
as spend their estates before they come to 'em, and are   300
cuckolds before they're married. But let me go look to my
own freehold—How!

Enter MY LADY FIDGET, MISTRESS DAINTY FIDGET
and MISTRESS SQUEAMISH

LADY FIDGET

Your servant, sir. Where is your lady? We are come to wait
upon her to the new play.

PINCHWIFE

New play!   305

LADY FIDGET

And my husband will wait upon you presently.

PINCHWIFE (*Aside*)

Damn your civility.—Madam, by no means; I will not see
Sir Jaspar here till I have waited upon him at home; nor shall
my wife see you till she has waited upon your ladyship at
your lodgings.   310

LADY FIDGET

Now we are here, sir. . . .

PINCHWIFE

No, madam.

DAINTY

Pray let us see her.

SQUEAMISH

We will not stir till we see her.

PINCHWIFE (*Aside*)

A pox on you all!   (*Goes to the door and returns*)   315
She has locked the door and is gone abroad.

LADY FIDGET

No, you have locked the door, and she's within.

297 *trimmings* clothes
307 s.d. (*Aside*) (omit Q3)

DAINTY
    They told us below, she was here.
PINCHWIFE [*Aside*]
    Will nothing do?—Well, it must out then. To tell you the
    truth, ladies, which I was afraid to let you know before, lest   320
    it might endanger your lives, my wife has just now the small-
    pox come out upon her. Do not be frightened; but pray, be
    gone, ladies; you shall not stay here in danger of your lives;
    pray get you gone, ladies.
LADY FIDGET
    No, no, we have all had 'em.   325
SQUEAMISH
    Alack, alack!
DAINTY
    Come, come, we must see how it goes with her; I understand
    the disease.
LADY FIDGET
    Come.
PINCHWIFE (*Aside*)
    Well, there is no being too hard for women at their own   330
    weapon, lying; therefore I'll quit the field.
                                                    Exit PINCHWIFE
SQUEAMISH
    Here's an example of jealousy!
LADY FIDGET
    Indeed, as the world goes, I wonder there are no more
    jealous, since wives are so neglected.
DAINTY
    Pshaw! as the world goes, to what end should they be   335
    jealous?
LADY FIDGET
    Foh! 'tis a nasty world.
SQUEAMISH
    That men of parts, great acquaintance, and quality should
    take up with and spend themselves and fortunes in keeping
    little playhouse creatures, foh!   340
LADY FIDGET
    Nay, that women of understanding, great acquaintance and
    good quality should fall a-keeping, too, of little creatures,
    foh!
SQUEAMISH
    Why, 'tis the men of quality's fault. They never visit women
    of honour and reputation as they used to do; and have not so   345

344 *women* (woman Q5)

much as common civility for ladies of our rank, but use us
with the same indifferency and ill-breeding as if we were all
married to 'em.

LADY FIDGET

She says true! 'Tis an arrant shame women of quality should
be so slighted. Methinks, birth—birth should go for some-　350
thing. I have known men admired, courted, and followed
for their titles only.

SQUEAMISH

Ay, one would think men of honour should not love, no more
than marry, out of their own rank.

DAINTY

Fie, fie upon 'em! They are come to think cross-breeding for　355
themselves best, as well as for their dogs and horses.

LADY FIDGET

They are dogs, and horses for't.

SQUEAMISH

One would think, if not for love, for vanity a little.

DAINTY

Nay, they do satisfy their vanity upon us sometimes, and are
kind to us in their report—tell all the world they live with us.　360

LADY FIDGET

Damned rascals! That we should be only wronged by 'em.
To report a man has had a person, when he has not had a
person, is the greatest wrong in the whole world that can be
done to a person.

SQUEAMISH

Well, 'tis an arrant shame noble persons should be so　365
wronged and neglected.

LADY FIDGET

But still 'tis an arranter shame for a noble person to neglect
her own honour, and defame her own noble person with
little inconsiderable fellows, foh!

DAINTY

I suppose the crime against our honour is the same with a　370
man of quality as with another.

LADY FIDGET

How! No, sure, the man of quality is likest one's husband,
and therefore the fault should be the less.

DAINTY

But then the pleasure should be the less!

LADY FIDGET

Fie, fie, fie, for shame, sister! Whither shall we ramble? Be　375
continent in your discourse, or I shall hate you.

R–C

DAINTY

Besides, an intrigue is so much the more notorious for the man's quality.

SQUEAMISH

'Tis true, nobody takes notice of a private man, and there-fore with him 'tis more secret, and the crime's the less when 380 'tis not known.

LADY FIDGET

You say true. I'faith, I think you are in the right on't. 'Tis not an injury to a husband till it be an injury to our honours; so that a woman of honour loses no honour with a private person—and to say truth. . . . 385

DAINTY (*Apart to* SQUEAMISH)

So, the little fellow is grown a private person . . . with her.

LADY FIDGET

But still my dear, dear honour.

Enter SIR JASPAR, HORNER, DORILANT

SIR JASPAR

Ay, my dear, dear of honour, thou hast still so much honour in thy mouth. . . .

HORNER (*Aside*)

That she has none elsewhere. 390

LADY FIDGET

Oh, what d'ye mean to bring in these upon us?

DAINTY

Foh! these are as bad as wits.

SQUEAMISH

Foh!

LADY FIDGET

Let us leave the room.

SIR JASPAR

Stay, stay; faith, to tell you the naked truth . . . 395

LADY FIDGET

Fie, Sir Jaspar, do not use that word *naked*.

SIR JASPAR

Well, well, in short, I have business at Whitehall, and cannot go to the play with you, therefore would have you go . . .

LADY FIDGET

With those two to a play?

383 *honours* (honour Q5)
396 *that* (the Q5)

SIR JASPAR

    No, not with t'other, but with Mr Horner. There can be no   400
more scandal to go with him than with Mr Tattle, or Master
Limberham.

LADY FIDGET

    With that nasty fellow! No!—no!

SIR JASPAR

    Nay, prithee dear, hear me.   *Whispers to* LADY FIDGET

HORNER

    Ladies. . . .   405

       HORNER, DORILANT *drawing near* SQUEAMISH *and* DAINTY

DAINTY

    Stand off!

SQUEAMISH

    Do not approach us!

DAINTY

    You herd with the wits, you are obscenity all over.

SQUEAMISH

    I would as soon look upon a picture of Adam and Eve, with-
out fig leaves, as any of you, if I could help it, therefore keep   410
off, and do not make us sick.

DORILANT

    What a devil are these?

HORNER

    Why, these are pretenders to honour, as critics to wit, only
by censuring others; and as every raw, peevish, out-of-
humoured, affected, dull, tea-drinking, arithmetical fop sets   415
up for a wit, by railing at men of sense, so these for honour by
railing at the court and ladies of as great honour as quality.

SIR JASPAR

    Come, Mr Horner, I must desire you to go with these ladies
to the play, sir.

HORNER

    I, sir?   420

401–02 *Mr Tattle, or Master Limberham* names for harmless gallants, the
    old boys of I.i, 188; the latter name apparently invented by Wycherley—
    see *O.E.D.*
415 *arithmetical* precise, suggesting over-precise

---

404 s.d. difficult to know what it is that Sir Jaspar tells his wife here, since
    he has already communicated Horner's secret (I.i,99). Maybe Wycherley
    forgot this business had already been done; perhaps he needed to allow
    Horner and Dorilant the centre of the stage for their brief encounter
    with Dainty and Squeamish

SIR JASPAR
  Ay, ay, come, sir.
HORNER
  I must beg your pardon, sir, and theirs. I will not be seen in
  women's company in public again for the world.
SIR JASPAR
  Ha, ha! strange aversion!
SQUEAMISH
  No, he's for women's company in private.   425
SIR JASPAR
  He—poor man—he! ha, ha, ha!
DAINTY
  'Tis a greater shame amongst lewd fellows to be seen in
  virtuous women's company than for the women to be seen
  with them.
HORNER
  Indeed, madam, the time was I only hated virtuous women,   430
  but now I hate the other too; I beg your pardon, ladies.
LADY FIDGET
  You are very obliging, sir, because we would not be troubled
  with you.
SIR JASPAR
  In sober sadness, he shall go.
DORILANT
  Nay, if he wo'not, I am ready to wait upon the ladies; and I 435
  think I am the fitter man.
SIR JASPAR
  You, sir, no, I thank you for that—Master Horner is a
  privileged man amongst the virtuous ladies; 'twill be a great
  while before you are so, he, he, he! He's my wife's gallant,
  he, he, he! No, pray withdraw, sir, for as I take it, the   440
  virtuous ladies have no business with you.
DORILANT
  And I am sure he can have none with them. 'Tis strange a
  man can't come amongst virtuous women now but upon the
  same terms as men are admitted into the great Turk's
  seraglio; but heaven keep me from being an ombre player   445
  with 'em! But where is Pinchwife?

                                              Exit DORILANT

---

445 *ombre* card game. The seventeenth-century spelling (*hombre*) suggests
   that Dorilant may be toying with the double meaning of not wanting to
   play at being a man

SIR JASPAR
Come, come, man; what, avoid the sweet society of womankind?—that sweet, soft, gentle, tame, noble creature, woman,
made for man's companion . . .

HORNER
So is that soft, gentle, tame, and more noble creature a 450
spaniel and has all their tricks—can fawn, lie down, suffer
beating, and fawn the more; barks at your friends when they
come to see you; makes your bed hard; gives you fleas, and
the mange sometimes. And all the difference is, the spaniel's
the more faithful animal and fawns but upon one master. 455

SIR JASPAR
He, he, he!

SQUEAMISH
Oh, the rude beast!

DAINTY
Insolent brute!

LADY FIDGET
Brute! Stinking, mortified, rotten French wether, to dare. . . .

SIR JASPAR
Hold, an't please your ladyship.—For shame, Master 460
Horner, your mother was a woman.—(*Aside*) Now shall I
never reconcile 'em.—Hark you, madam, take my advice in
your anger. You know you often want one to make up your
drolling pack of ombre players; and you may cheat him
easily, for he's an ill gamester, and consequently loves play. 465
Besides, you know, you have but two old civil gentlemen
(with stinking breaths too) to wait upon you abroad; take in
the third into your service. The other are but crazy; and a
lady should have a supernumerary gentleman-usher, as a
supernumerary coachhorse, lest sometimes you should be 470
forced to stay at home.

LADY FIDGET
But are you sure he loves play, and has money?

SIR JASPAR
He loves play as much as you, and has money as much as I.

LADY FIDGET
Then I am contented to make him pay for his scurrility;
money makes up in a measure all other wants in men.— 475

459 *mortified* dead
   wether castrated ram. Here, a man made impotent by the French pox
464 *drolling* comic, clownish
468 *crazy* frail, sickly
469 *gentleman-usher* escort

(*Aside*) Those whom we cannot make hold for gallants, we make fine.

SIR JASPAR (*Aside*)
So, so; now to mollify, to wheedle him.—Master Horner, will you never keep civil company? Methinks 'tis time now, since you are only fit for them. Come, come, man, you must   480 e'en fall to visiting our wives, eating at our tables, drinking tea with our virtuous relations after dinner, dealing cards to 'em, reading plays and gazettes to 'em, picking fleas out of their shocks for 'em, collecting receipts, new songs, women, pages, and footmen for 'em.   485

HORNER
I hope they'll afford me better employment, sir.

SIR JASPAR
He, he, he! 'Tis fit you know your work before you come into our place; and since you are unprovided of a lady to flatter, and a good house to eat at, pray frequent mine, and call my wife mistress, and she shall call you gallant, according to the   490 custom.

HORNER
Who, I?

SIR JASPAR
Faith, thou shalt for my sake; come, for my sake only.

HORNER
For your sake. . . .

SIR JASPAR
Come, come, here's a gamester for you; let him be a little   495 familiar sometimes; nay, what if a little rude? Gamesters may be rude with ladies, you know.

LADY FIDGET
Yes, losing gamesters have a privilege with women.

HORNER
I always thought the contrary, that the winning gamester had most privilege with women; for when you have lost your   500 money to a man, you'll lose anything you have, all you have, they say, and he may use you as he pleases.

477 *fine* pay
478 *wheedle* swindle
484 *shocks* poodles
    receipts recipes

---

477 *fine* Gerald Weales suggests that this is especially relevant here because the verb was generally used to refer to the fines men paid to avoid the duties of an office—and Horner cannot presumably carry out one of the usual duties of a gallant

SIR JASPAR

He, he, he! Well, win or lose, you shall have your liberty with
her.

LADY FIDGET

As he behaves himself; and for your sake I'll give him   505
admittance and freedom.

HORNER

All sorts of freedom, madam?

SIR JASPAR

Ay, ay, ay, all sorts of freedom thou canst take, and so go to
her, begin thy new employment; wheedle her, jest with her,
and be better acquainted one with another.   510

HORNER (*Aside*)

I think I know her already, therefore may venture with her,
my secret for hers.   HORNER *and* LADY FIDGET *whisper*

SIR JASPAR

Sister, cuz, I have provided an innocent playfellow for you
there.

DAINTY

Who, he!   515

SQUEAMISH

There's a playfellow indeed!

SIR JASPAR

Yes, sure, what, he is good enough to play at cards, blind-
man's buff, or the fool with sometimes.

SQUEAMISH

Foh! we'll have no such playfellows.

DAINTY

No, sir, you shan't choose playfellows for us, we thank you.   520

SIR JASPAR

Nay, pray hear me.   *Whispering to them*

LADY FIDGET

But, poor gentleman, could you be so generous, so truly a
man of honour, as for the sakes of us women of honour, to
cause yourself to be reported no man? No man! And to
suffer yourself the greatest shame that could fall upon a man,   525
that none might fall upon us women by your conversation?
But indeed, sir, as perfectly, perfectly, the same man as
before going into France, sir? As perfectly, perfectly, sir?

511 *venture* Q2–5, 0 (venter Q1)

---

521 s.d. presumably persuading them, as he did his wife, how they can win
off Horner at cards, etc.

HORNER

As perfectly, perfectly, madam. Nay, I scorn you should take my word; I desire to be tried only, madam. 530

LADY FIDGET

Well, that's spoken again like a man of honour; all men of honour desire to come to the test. But, indeed, generally, you men report such things of yourselves, one does not know how or whom to believe; and it is come to that pass we dare not take your words no more than your tailor's, without 535 some staid servant of yours be bound with you. But I have so strong a faith in your honour, dear, dear, noble sir, that I'd forfeit mine for yours at any time, dear sir.

HORNER

No, madam, you should not need to forfeit it for me. I have given you security already to save you harmless, my late 540 reputation being so well known in the world, madam.

LADY FIDGET

But if upon any future falling out, or upon a suspicion of my taking the trust out of your hands, to employ some other, you yourself should betray your trust, dear sir? I mean, if you'll give me leave to speak obscenely, you might tell, dear 545 sir.

HORNER

If I did, nobody would believe me! The reputation of impotency is as hardly recovered again in the world as that of cowardice, dear madam.

LADY FIDGET

Nay, then, as one may say, you may do your worst, dear, 550 dear, sir.

SIR JASPAR

Come, is your ladyship reconciled to him yet? Have you agreed on matters? For I must be gone to Whitehall.

LADY FIDGET

Why, indeed, Sir Jaspar, Master Horner is a thousand, thousand times a better man than I thought him. Cousin 555 Squeamish, Sister Dainty, I can name him now, truly; not long ago, you know, I thought his very name obscenity, and I would as soon have lain with him as have named him.

SIR JASPAR

Very likely, poor madam.

536 *staid* (maid Q3)
    be bound with you testifying on your behalf
540 *save you harmless* secure you from harm by scandal
545 *obscenely* openly

DAINTY

  I believe it.   560

SQUEAMISH

  No doubt on't.

SIR JASPAR

  Well, well—that your ladyship is as virtuous as any she, I
  know, and him all the town knows—he, he, he! Therefore,
  now you like him, get you gone to your business together;
  go, go, to your business, I say, pleasure, whilst I go to my   565
  pleasure, business.

LADY FIDGET

  Come then, dear gallant.

HORNER

  Come away, my dearest mistress.

SIR JASPAR

  So, so; why 'tis as I'd have it.   *Exit* SIR JASPAR

HORNER

  And as I'd have it!   570

LADY FIDGET

  Who for his business from his wife will run,
  Takes the best care to have her business done!

                                                  Exeunt omnes

Act III, Scene i

ALITHEA *and* MRS PINCHWIFE

ALITHEA

  Sister, what ails you? You are grown melancholy.

MRS PINCHWIFE

  Would it not make anyone melancholy, to see you go every
  day fluttering about abroad, whilst I must stay at home like a
  poor, lonely, sullen bird in a cage?

ALITHEA

  Ay, sister, but you came young and just from the nest to your   5
  cage, so that I thought you liked it; and could be as cheerful
  in't as others that took their flight themselves early, and are
  hopping abroad in the open air.

MRS PINCHWIFE

  Nay, I confess I was quiet enough till my husband told me
  what pure lives the London ladies live abroad, with their   10
  dancing, meetings, and junketings, and dressed every day in
  their best gowns; and I warrant you, play at ninepins every
  day of the week, so they do.

                        Enter MR PINCHWIFE

10 *pure* fine

PINCHWIFE
> Come, what's here to do? You are putting the town pleasures
> in her head, and setting her a-longing. 15

ALITHEA
> Yes, after ninepins! You suffer none to give her those
> longings, you mean, but yourself.

PINCHWIFE
> I tell her of the vanities of the town like a confessor.

ALITHEA
> A confessor! Just such a confessor as he that, by forbidding a
> silly ostler to grease the horse's teeth, taught him to do't. 20

PINCHWIFE
> Come, Mistress Flippant, good precepts are lost when bad
> examples are still before us. The liberty you take abroad
> makes her hanker after it, and out of humour at home. Poor
> wretch! she desired not to come to London; I would bring
> her. 25

ALITHEA
> Very well.

PINCHWIFE
> She has been this week in town, and never desired, till this
> afternoon, to go abroad.

ALITHEA
> Was she not at a play yesterday?

PINCHWIFE
> Yes, but she ne'er asked me. I was myself the cause of her 30
> going.

ALITHEA
> Then, if she ask you again, you are the cause of her asking,
> and not my example.

PINCHWIFE
> Well, tomorrow night I shall be rid of you; and the next day,
> before 'tis light, she and I'll be rid of the town, and my 35
> dreadful apprehensions. Come, be not melancholy, for thou
> shalt go into the country after tomorrow, dearest.

ALITHEA
> Great comfort!

MRS PINCHWIFE
> Pish! what d'ye tell me of the country for?

PINCHWIFE
> How's this! What, pish at the country? 40

15 *setting* (set Q5)
20 *silly* ignorant

MRS PINCHWIFE

Let me alone, I am not well.

PINCHWIFE

O, if that be all—what ails my dearest?

MRS PINCHWIFE

Truly I don't know; but I have not been well since you told
me there was a gallant at the play in love with me.

PINCHWIFE

Ha!   45

ALITHEA

That's by my example, too!

PINCHWIFE

Nay, if you are not well, but are so concerned because a lewd
fellow chanced to lie and say he liked you, you'll make me
sick too.

MRS PINCHWIFE

Of what sickness?   50

PINCHWIFE

O, of that which is worse than the plague—jealousy.

MRS PINCHWIFE

Pish, you jeer! I'm sure there's no such disease in our
receipt-book at home.

PINCHWIFE

No, thou never met'st with it, poor innocent. (*Aside*) Well, if
thou cuckold me, 'twill be my own fault, for cuckolds and   55
bastards are generally makers of their own fortune.

MRS PINCHWIFE

Well, but pray, bud, let's go to a play tonight.

PINCHWIFE

'Tis just done, she comes from it; but why are you so eager
to see a play?

MRS PINCHWIFE

Faith, dear, not that I care one pin for their talk there, but I   60
like to look upon the player-men, and would see, if I could,
the gallant you say loves me; that's all, dear bud.

PINCHWIFE

Is that all, dear bud?

ALITHEA

This proceeds from my example.

MRS PINCHWIFE

But if the play be done, let's go abroad, however, dear bud.   65

PINCHWIFE

Come, have a little patience, and thou shalt go into the
country on Friday.

MRS PINCHWIFE

Therefore I would see first some sights, to tell my neighbours of. Nay, I will go abroad, that's once.

ALITHEA

I'm the cause of this desire too.   70

PINCHWIFE

But now I think on't, who was the cause of Horner's coming to my lodging today? That was you.

ALITHEA

No, you, because you would not let him see your handsome wife out of your lodging.

MRS PINCHWIFE

Why, O lord! did the gentleman come hither to see me   75
indeed?

PINCHWIFE

No, no.—You are not cause of that damned question too, Mistress Alithea? (*Aside*) Well, she's in the right of it. He is in love with my wife . . . and comes after her . . . 'tis so . . . but I'll nip his love in the bud; lest he should follow us into the   80
country, and break his chariot-wheel near our house on purpose for an excuse to come to't. But I think I know the town.

MRS PINCHWIFE

Come, pray bud, let's go abroad before 'tis late. For I will go, that's flat and plain.   85

PINCHWIFE (*Aside*)

So! the obstinacy already of a town-wife, and I must, whilst she's here, humour her like one.—Sister, how shall we do, that she may not be seen or known?

ALITHEA

Let her put on her mask.

PINCHWIFE

Pshaw! A mask makes people but the more inquisitive, and   90
is as ridiculous a disguise as a stage beard; her shape, stature, habit will be known. And if we should meet with Horner, he would be sure to take acquaintance with us, must wish her joy, kiss her, talk to her, leer upon her, and the devil and all. No, I'll not use her to a mask, 'tis dangerous; for masks have   95
made more cuckolds than the best faces that ever were known.

69 *once* once for all
71 *who* Q1 (who, who Q2–5, 0)
77 *cause* Q1–3 (the cause Q4–5, 0)
86 *a* Q1 (the Q2–5, 0)

ALITHEA

How will you do then?

MRS PINCHWIFE

Nay, shall we go? The Exchange will be shut, and I have a
mind to see that. 100

PINCHWIFE

So . . . I have it. . . . I'll dress her up in the suit we are to
carry down to her brother, little Sir James; nay, I understand the town tricks. Come, let's go dress her. A mask! No
—a woman masked, like a covered dish, gives a man curiosity
and appetite, when, it may be, uncovered, 'twould turn his 105
stomach; no, no.

ALITHEA

Indeed your comparison is something a greasy one. But I had a
gentle gallant used to say, 'A beauty masked, like the sun in
eclipse, gathered together more gazers than if it shined out'.

Exeunt

[Act III, Scene ii]

The Scene changes to the New Exchange

Enter HORNER, HARCOURT, DORILANT

DORILANT

Engaged to women, and not sup with us?

HORNER

Ay, a pox on 'em all.

HARCOURT

You were much a more reasonable man in the morning, and
had as noble resolutions against 'em as a widower of a week's
liberty. 5

DORILANT

Did I ever think to see you keep company with women in
vain?

HORNER

In vain! No—'tis, since I can't love 'em, to be revenged on
'em.

HARCOURT

Now your sting is gone, you looked in the box, amongst all 10
those women, like a drone in the hive, all upon you; shoved
and ill-used by 'em all, and thrust from one side to t'other.

107 *greasy* filthy, obscene, with pun on greasy dishes
108 *like* Q2–5, 0 (lik'd Q1)

DORILANT

Yet he must be buzzing amongst 'em still, like other old
beetle-headed, lickerish drones. Avoid 'em, and hate 'em as
they hate you.   15

HORNER

Because I do hate 'em and would hate 'em yet more, I'll
frequent 'em. You may see by marriage, nothing makes a
man hate a woman more, than her constant conversation. In
short, I converse with 'em, as you do with rich fools, to laugh
at 'em and use 'em ill.   20

DORILANT

But I would no more sup with women, unless I could lie
with 'em, than sup with a rich coxcomb, unless I could cheat
him.

HORNER

Yes, I have known thee sup with a fool for his drinking; if he
could set out your hand that way only, you were satisfied, and   25
if he were a wine-swallowing mouth 'twas enough.

HARCOURT

Yes, a man drinks often with a fool, as he tosses with a
marker, only to keep his hand in ure. But do the ladies
drink?

HORNER

Yes, sir, and I shall have the pleasure at least of laying 'em   30
flat with a bottle, and bring as much scandal that way upon
'em as formerly t'other.

HARCOURT

Perhaps you may prove as weak a brother amongst 'em that
way as t'other.

DORILANT

Foh! drinking with women is as unnatural as scolding with   35
'em. But 'tis a pleasure of decayed fornicators, and the basest
way of quenching love.

---

14 *beetle-headed* stupid
   lickerish lecherous
27 *tosses* throws (dice)
28 *marker* scorekeeper in dice game
   ure practice
33–4 *that way as* (as formerly Q5)

---

25 *set out your hand* this is perhaps explained by Harcourt's following
   remark: you gain from him. There's a possible allusion to cards or dice
   too, but the main implication is that a man drinks with a fool to keep in
   practice at imbibing

HARCOURT

Nay, 'tis drowning love instead of quenching it. But leave us
for civil women too!

DORILANT

Ay, when he can't be the better for 'em. We hardly pardon   40
a man that leaves his friend for a wench, and that's a pretty
lawful call.

HORNER

Faith, I would not leave you for 'em, if they would not drink.

DORILANT

Who would disappoint his company at Lewis's for a
gossiping?   45

HARCOURT

Foh! Wine and women, good apart, together as nauseous as
sack and sugar. But hark you, sir, before you go, a little of
your advice; an old maimed general, when unfit for action, is
fittest for counsel. I have other designs upon women than
eating and drinking with them. I am in love with Sparkish's   50
mistress, whom he is to marry tomorrow. Now how shall I get
her?

Enter SPARKISH, *looking about*

HORNER

Why, here comes one will help you to her.

HARCOURT

He! He, I tell you, is my rival, and will hinder my love.

HORNER

No, a foolish rival and a jealous husband assist their rival's   55
designs; for they are sure to make their women hate them,
which is the first step to their love for another man.

HARCOURT

But I cannot come near his mistress but in his company.

HORNER

Still the better for you, for fools are most easily cheated
when they themselves are accessories; and he is to be   60
bubbled of his mistress, as of his money, the common
mistress, by keeping him company.

SPARKISH

Who is that, that is to be bubbled? Faith, let me snack, I
han't met with a bubble since Christmas. Gad, I think

39 *civil women* i.e., not wenches
44 *Lewis's* a London tavern
47 *sack* a Spanish wine (like sherry) which presumably—*pace* Falstaff—
   was not improved by adding sugar
61 *bubbled* gulled
63 *snack* share

bubbles are like their brother woodcocks, go out with the   65
cold weather.

HARCOURT (*Apart to* HORNER)

A pox! he did not hear all I hope.

SPARKISH

Come, you bubbling rogues you, where do we sup?—Oh,
Harcourt, my mistress tells me you have been making fierce
love to her all the play long, ha, ha!—But I . . .   70

HARCOURT

I make love to her?

SPARKISH

Nay, I forgive thee; for I think I know thee, and I know her,
but I am sure I know myself.

HARCOURT

Did she tell you so? I see all women are like these of the
Exchange, who, to enhance the price of their commodities,   75
report to their fond customers offers which were never made
'em.

HORNER

Ay, women are as apt to tell before the intrigue as men after
it, and so show themselves the vainer sex. But hast thou a
mistress, Sparkish? 'Tis as hard for me to believe it as that   80
thou ever hadst a bubble, as you bragged just now.

SPARKISH

Oh, your servant, sir; are you at your raillery, sir? But we
were some of us beforehand with you today at the play. The
wits were something bold with you, sir; did you not hear us
laugh?   85

HARCOURT

Yes, but I thought you had gone to plays to laugh at the
poet's wit, not at your own.

SPARKISH

Your servant, sir; no, I thank you. Gad, I go to a play as to a
country treat. I carry my own wine to one, and my own wit to
t'other, or else I'm sure I should not be merry at either. And   90
the reason why we are so often louder than the players is
because we think we speak more wit, and so become the
poet's rivals in his audience. For to tell you the truth, we
hate the silly rogues; nay, so much that we find fault even
with their bawdy upon the stage, whilst we talk nothing else   95
in the pit as loud.

65 *woodcocks* simpletons
78 *as apt* Q1 (apt Q2–5, 0)
81 *bragged* (barg'd Q5)
84 *were* Q1 (are Q2–5, 0)

HORNER

But, why should'st thou hate the silly poets? Thou hast too
much wit to be one, and they, like whores, are only hated by
each other. And thou dost scorn writing, I'm sure.

SPARKISH

Yes, I'd have you to know, I scorn writing. But women,   100
women, that make men do all foolish things, make 'em write
songs too. Everybody does it. 'Tis even as common with
lovers as playing with fans; and you can no more help
rhyming to your Phyllis than drinking to your Phyllis.

HARCOURT

Nay, poetry in love is no more to be avoided than jealousy.   105

DORILANT

But the poets damned your songs, did they?

SPARKISH

Damn the poets! They turned 'em into burlesque, as they
call it. That burlesque is a hocus-pocus trick they have got,
which by the virtue of hictius doctius, topsy-turvy, they
make a wise and witty man in the world a fool upon the   110
stage, you know not how.—And 'tis therefore I hate 'em too,
for I know not but it may be my own case; for they'll put a
man into a play for looking asquint. Their predecessors were
contented to make serving-men only their stage-fools, but
these rogues must have gentlemen, with a pox to 'em, nay   115
knights. And, indeed, you shall hardly see a fool upon the
stage but he's a knight. And to tell you the truth, they have
kept me these six years from being a knight in earnest, for
fear of being knighted in a play, and dubbed a fool.

DORILANT

Blame 'em not, they must follow their copy—the age.   120

HARCOURT

But why should'st thou be afraid of being in a play, who
expose yourself every day in the playhouses, and as public
places?

HORNER

'Tis but being on the stage, instead of standing on a bench in
the pit.   125

DORILANT

Don't you give money to painters to draw you like? And are
you afraid of your pictures at length in a playhouse, where all
your mistresses may see you?

109 *hictius doctius* (hixius doxius Q5) a term used by jugglers
120 *their* (in their Q5)
122 *as* Q1–2 (at Q3–5, 0) equally

SPARKISH
  A pox! Painters don't draw the smallpox or pimples in one's
  face. Come, damn all your silly authors whatever, all books   130
  and booksellers, by the world, and all readers, courteous or
  uncourteous.
HARCOURT
  But, who comes here, Sparkish?
          Enter MR PINCHWIFE *and his wife in man's clothes,*
                    ALITHEA, LUCY *her maid*
SPARKISH
  Oh hide me! There's my mistress too.
                    SPARKISH *hides himself behind* HARCOURT
HARCOURT
  She sees you.   135
SPARKISH
  But I will not see her. 'Tis time to go to Whitehall, and I
  must not fail the drawing-room.
HARCOURT
  Pray, first carry me, and reconcile me to her.
SPARKISH
  Another time! Faith, the king will have supped.
HARCOURT
  Not with the worse stomach for thy absence! Thou art one   140
  of those fools that think their attendance at the king's meals
  as necessary as his physicians', when you are more trouble-
  some to him than his doctors, or his dogs.
SPARKISH
  Pshaw! I know my interest, sir. Prithee, hide me.
HORNER
  Your servant, Pinchwife.—What, he knows us not!   145
PINCHWIFE (*To his wife, aside*)
  Come along.
MRS PINCHWIFE
  Pray, have you any ballads? Give me sixpenny worth?
CLASP
  We have no ballads.
MRS PINCHWIFE
  Then give me *Covent Garden Drollery* and a play or two. . . .
  Oh, here's *Tarugo's Wiles* and *The Slighted Maiden*. I'll have 150
  them.

---

148 s.p. CLASP a vendor not listed among *The Persons* (above, p. 5)

149–50 *Covent Garden Drollery* was a compilation by Alexander Brome of
    songs, prologues, and epilogues from plays, published in 1672. *Tarugo's
    Wiles* (1668) was a comedy by Sir Thomas St Serfe, and *The Slighted
    Maiden* (1663), a comedy by Sir Robert Stapleton.

PINCHWIFE (*Apart to her*)

No, plays are not for your reading. Come along; will you discover yourself?

HORNER

Who is that pretty youth with him, Sparkish?

SPARKISH

I believe his wife's brother, because he's something like her;   155
but I never saw her but once.

HORNER

Extremely handsome. I have seen a face like it too. Let us follow 'em.

Exeunt PINCHWIFE, MISTRESS PINCHWIFE,
ALITHEA, LUCY; HORNER, DORILANT *following them*

HARCOURT

Come, Sparkish, your mistress saw you, and will be angry you go not to her. Besides I would fain be reconciled to her,   160
which none but you can do, dear friend.

SPARKISH

Well, that's a better reason, dear friend. I would not go near her now, for hers or my own sake, but I can deny you nothing; for though I have known thee a great while, never go, if I do not love thee as well as a new acquaintance.   165

HARCOURT

I am obliged to you indeed, dear friend. I would be well with her, only to be well with thee still; for these ties to wives usually dissolve all ties to friends. I would be contented she should enjoy you a-nights, but I would have you to myself a-days, as I have had, dear friend.   170

SPARKISH

And thou shalt enjoy me a-days, dear, dear friend, never stir; and I'll be divorced from her, sooner than from thee. Come along . . .

HARCOURT (*Aside*)

So we are hard put to't, when we make our rival our pro-curer; but neither she nor her brother would let me come   175
near her now. When all's done, a rival is the best cloak to steal to a mistress under, without suspicion; and when we have once got to her as we desire, we throw him off like other cloaks.

Exit SPARKISH, *and* HARCOURT *following him*
Re-enter MR PINCHWIFE, MISTRESS PINCHWIFE *in*
man's clothes

171 *dear, dear friend* Q1–2, Q4, 0 (dear Friend Q3, Q5)
171 *stir* fret
176 *near* (wear Q4)

PINCHWIFE (*To* ALITHEA [*off-stage*])

> Sister, if you will not go, we must leave you. (*Aside*) The   180
> fool her gallant and she will muster up all the young
> saunterers of this place, and they will leave their dear
> seamstresses to follow us. What a swarm of cuckolds and
> cuckold-makers are here!—Come, let's be gone, Mistress
> Margery.   185

MRS PINCHWIFE

> Don't you believe that, I han't half my bellyfull of sights yet.

PINCHWIFE

> Then walk this way.

MRS PINCHWIFE

> Lord, what a power of brave signs are here! Stay—the Bull's
> Head, the Ram's Head, and the Stag's Head! Dear . . .

PINCHWIFE

> Nay, if every husband's proper sign here were visible, they   190
> would be all alike.

MRS PINCHWIFE

> What d'ye mean by that, bud?

PINCHWIFE

> 'Tis no matter . . . no matter, bud.

MRS PINCHWIFE

> Pray tell me; nay, I will know.

PINCHWIFE

> They would all be bulls', stags', and rams' heads!   195

> > *Exeunt* MR PINCHWIFE, MRS PINCHWIFE

Re-enter SPARKISH, HARCOURT, ALITHEA, LUCY *at t'other door*

SPARKISH

> Come, dear madam, for my sake you shall be reconciled to
> him.

ALITHEA

> For your sake I hate him.

HARCOURT

> That's something too cruel, madam, to hate me for his sake.

SPARKISH

> Ay indeed, madam, too, too cruel to me, to hate my friend for   200
> my sake.

ALITHEA

> I hate him because he is your enemy; and you ought to hate
> him too, for making love to me, if you love me.

190 *husband's proper sign* cuckold's horns

---

195 s.d. *other door* there were two doors side by side on each side of the
stage

SPARKISH

That's a good one; I hate a man for loving you! If he did
love you, 'tis but what he can't help; and 'tis your fault not   205
his if he admires you. I hate a man for being of my opinion.
I'll ne'er do it, by the world.

ALITHEA

Is it for your honour or mine, to suffer a man to make love to
me, who am to marry you tomorrow?

SPARKISH

Is it for your honour or mine, to have me jealous? That he   210
makes love to you is a sign you are handsome; and that I am
not jealous, is a sign you are virtuous. That, I think, is for
your honour.

ALITHEA

But 'tis your honour too I am concerned for.

HARCOURT

But why, dearest madam, will you be more concerned for his   215
honour than he is himself? Let his honour alone, for my
sake and his. He, he has no honour . . .

SPARKISH

How's that?

HARCOURT

But what my dear friend can guard himself.

SPARKISH

O ho—that's right again.   220

HARCOURT

Your care of his honour argues his neglect of it, which is no
honour to my dear friend here; therefore once more, let his
honour go which way it will, dear madam.

SPARKISH

Ay, ay, were it for my honour to marry a woman whose
virtue I suspected, and could not trust her in a friend's   225
hands?

ALITHEA

Are you not afraid to lose me?

HARCOURT

He afraid to lose you, madam! No, no—you may see how the
most estimable and most glorious creature in the world is
valued by him. Will you not see it?   230

SPARKISH

Right, honest Frank, I have that noble value for her that I
cannot be jealous of her.

231 *Right, honest Frank* (Right honest Frank Q3)

ALITHEA

You mistake him. He means you care not for me nor who
has me.

SPARKISH

Lord, madam, I see you are jealous! Will you wrest a poor   235
man's meaning from his words?

ALITHEA

You astonish me, sir, with your want of jealousy.

SPARKISH

And you make me giddy, madam, with your jealousy and
fears, and virtue and honour. Gad, I see virtue makes a
woman as troublesome as a little reading or learning.   240

ALITHEA

Monstrous!

LUCY (*Behind*)

Well, to see what easy husbands these women of quality can
meet with! A poor chambermaid can never have such lady-
like luck. Besides, he's thrown away upon her; she'll make no
use of her fortune, her blessing; none to a gentleman for a   245
pure cuckold, for it requires good breeding to be a cuckold.

ALITHEA

I tell you then plainly, he pursues me to marry me.

SPARKISH

Pshaw!

HARCOURT

Come, madam, you see you strive in vain to make him
jealous of me. My dear friend is the kindest creature in the   250
world to me.

SPARKISH

Poor fellow.

HARCOURT

But his kindness only is not enough for me, without your
favour. Your good opinion, dear madam, 'tis that must
perfect my happiness. Good gentleman, he believes all I say;   255
would you would do so. Jealous of me! I would not wrong
him nor you for the world.

                    ALITHEA *walks carelessly to and fro*

SPARKISH

Look you there; hear him, hear him, and do not walk away
so.

235 *jealous* wrought up, feeling vehemently. Alithea plays upon its other
    sense of 'possessive' in the next speech
253 *only* (omit Q3)
257 s.d. *carelessly* without caring, unconcernedly

HARCOURT

I love you, madam, so ...   260

SPARKISH

How's that! Nay—now you begin to go too far indeed.

HARCOURT

So much, I confess, I say I love you, that I would not have
you miserable, and cast yourself away upon so unworthy and
inconsiderable a thing as what you see here.

> *Clapping his hand on his breast, points at* SPARKISH

SPARKISH

No, faith, I believe thou would'st not. Now his meaning is   265
plain. But I knew before thou would'st not wrong me nor
her.

HARCOURT

No, no, heavens forbid the glory of her sex should fall so low
as into the embraces of such a contemptible wretch, the last
of mankind—my dear friend here—I injure him.   270

> *Embracing* SPARKISH

ALITHEA

Very well.

SPARKISH

No, no, dear friend, I knew it. Madam, you see he will rather
wrong himself than me, in giving himself such names.

ALITHEA

Do not you understand him yet?

SPARKISH

Yes, how modestly he speaks of himself, poor fellow.   275

ALITHEA

Methinks he speaks impudently of yourself, since—before
yourself too; insomuch that I can no longer suffer his
scurrilous abusiveness to you, no more than his love to me.

> *Offers to go*

SPARKISH

Nay, nay, madam, pray stay. His love to you! Lord, madam,
has he not spoke yet plain enough?   280

ALITHEA

Yes indeed, I should think so.

SPARKISH

Well then, by the world, a man can't speak civilly to a woman
now but presently she says he makes love to her! Nay,
madam, you shall stay, with your pardon, since you have not
yet understood him, till he has made an eclaircissement of   285

269 *last* Q1 (least Q2–5, 0)
285 *eclaircissement* elucidation. An affectation

his love to you, that is, what kind of love it is. [*To* HARCOURT]
Answer to thy catechism: friend, do you love my mistress
here?

HARCOURT
Yes, I wish she would not doubt it.

SPARKISH
But how do you love her?   290

HARCOURT
With all my soul.

ALITHEA
I thank him; methinks he speaks plain enough now.

SPARKISH (*To* ALITHEA)
You are out still.—But with what kind of love, Harcourt?

HARCOURT
With the best and truest love in the world.

SPARKISH
Look you there then, that is with no matrimonial love, I'm   295
sure.

ALITHEA
How's that? Do you say matrimonial love is not best?

SPARKISH [*Aside*]
Gad, I went too far ere I was aware.—But speak for thyself,
Harcourt; you said you would not wrong me nor her.

HARCOURT
No, no, madam, e'en take him for heaven's sake. . . .   300

SPARKISH
Look you there, madam.

HARCOURT
Who should in all justice be yours, he that loves you most.
                                        Claps his hand on his breast

ALITHEA
Look you there, Mr Sparkish, who's that?

SPARKISH
Who should it be?—Go on, Harcourt.

HARCOURT
Who loves you more than women, titles, or fortune fools.   305
                                        Points at SPARKISH

SPARKISH
Look you there, he means me still, for he points at me.

ALITHEA
Ridiculous!

HARCOURT
Who can only match your faith and constancy in love.

298 s.d. [*Aside*] yet maybe he *is* foolish enough to speak openly

SPARKISH
Ay.

HARCOURT
Who knows, if it be possible, how to value so much beauty   310
and virtue.

SPARKISH
Ay.

HARCOURT
Whose love can no more be equalled in the world than that
heavenly form of yours.

SPARKISH
No.   315

HARCOURT
Who could no more suffer a rival than your absence, and yet
could no more suspect your virtue than his own constancy in
his love to you.

SPARKISH
No.

HARCOURT
Who, in fine, loves you better than his eyes, that first made   320
him love you.

SPARKISH
Ay—nay, madam, faith, you shan't go, till . . .

ALITHEA
Have a care, lest you make me stay too long. . . .

SPARKISH
But till he has saluted you; that I may be assured you are
friends, after his honest advice and declaration. Come, pray,   325
madam, be friends with him.

Enter MASTER PINCHWIFE, MISTRESS PINCHWIFE

ALITHEA
You must pardon me, sir, that I am not yet so obedient to
you.

PINCHWIFE
What, invite your wife to kiss men? Monstrous! Are you not
ashamed? I will never forgive you.   330

SPARKISH
Are you not ashamed that I should have more confidence in
the chastity of your family than you have? You must not

313 *no more be* (be no more Q5)
320 *in fine* in short
324 *he* (she Q5)
325 *his* (this Q5)

teach me, I am a man of honour, sir, though I am frank and
free. I am frank, sir. . . .

PINCHWIFE
Very frank, sir, to share your wife with your friends. 335

SPARKISH
He is an humble, menial friend, such as reconciles the
differences of the marriage bed. You know man and wife do
not always agree; I design him for that use, therefore would
have him well with my wife.

PINCHWIFE
A menial friend! You will get a great many menial friends by 340
showing your wife as you do.

SPARKISH
What then? It may be I have a pleasure in't, as I have to show
fine clothes at a playhouse the first day, and count money
before poor rogues.

PINCHWIFE
He that shows his wife or money will be in danger of having 345
them borrowed sometimes.

SPARKISH
I love to be envied, and would not marry a wife that I alone
could love. Loving alone is as dull as eating alone. Is it not a
frank age? And I am a frank person. And to tell you the truth,
it may be I love to have rivals in a wife; they make her seem 350
to a man still but as a kept mistress. And so good night, for I
must to Whitehall. Madam, I hope you are now reconciled to
my friend; and so I wish you a good night, madam, and
sleep if you can, for tomorrow you know I must visit you early
with a canonical gentleman. Good night, dear Harcourt. 355
Exit SPARKISH

HARCOURT
Madam, I hope you will not refuse my visit tomorrow, if it
should be earlier with a canonical gentleman than Mr
Sparkish's.

PINCHWIFE (*Coming between* ALITHEA *and* HARCOURT)
This gentlewoman is yet under my care; therefore you must
yet forbear your freedom with her, sir. 360

HARCOURT
Must, sir!

PINCHWIFE
Yes, sir, she is my sister.

333 *frank* open, candid. In the following speech Pinchwife plays upon its
meaning of 'generous'
336 *menial* domestic, in the house
358 *Sparkish's* (Sparkish Q3)

HARCOURT

'Tis well she is, sir—for I must be her servant, sir.
Madam . . .

PINCHWIFE

Come away, sister. We had been gone if it had not been for   365
you, and so avoided these lewd rakehells, who seem to haunt
us.

Enter HORNER, DORILANT *to them*

HORNER

How now, Pinchwife!

PINCHWIFE

Your servant.

HORNER

What! I see a little time in the country makes a man turn   370
wild and unsociable, and only fit to converse with his
horses, dogs, and his herds.

PINCHWIFE

I have business, sir, and must mind it. Your business is
pleasure, therefore you and I must go different ways.

HORNER

Well, you may go on, but this pretty young gentleman . . .   375
Takes hold of MRS PINCHWIFE

HARCOURT

The lady . . .

DORILANT

And the maid . . .

HORNER

Shall stay with us, for I suppose their business is the same
with ours—pleasure.

PINCHWIFE (*Aside*)

'Sdeath, he knows her, she carries it so sillily! Yet if he does   380
not, I should be more silly to discover it first.

ALITHEA

Pray, let us go, sir.

PINCHWIFE

Come, come.

HORNER (*To* MRS PINCHWIFE)

Had you not rather stay with us?—Prithee, Pinchwife, who is
this pretty young gentleman?   385

366 *lewd* (omit Q)5
     rakehells rakes
372 *herds* (herd Q5)
385 *this* (that Q5)

PINCHWIFE

One to whom I'm a guardian. (*Aside*) I wish I could keep her out of your hands.

HORNER

Who is he? I never saw anything so pretty in all my life.

PINCHWIFE

Pshaw! do not look upon him so much; he's a poor bashful youth, you'll put him out of countenance. Come away, 390
brother.   *Offers to take her away*

HORNER

Oh, your brother?

PINCHWIFE

Yes, my wife's brother. Come, come, she'll stay supper for us.

HORNER

I thought so, for he is very like her I saw you at the play 395
with, whom I told you I was in love with.

MRS PINCHWIFE (*Aside*)

O jeminy! Is this he that was in love with me? I am glad on't, I vow, for he's a curious fine gentleman, and I love him already too. (*To* MR PINCHWIFE) Is this he, bud?

PINCHWIFE (*To his wife*)

Come away, come away!   400

HORNER

Why, what haste are you in? Why won't you let me talk with him?

PINCHWIFE

Because you'll debauch him. He's yet young and innocent, and I would not have him debauched for anything in the world. (*Aside*) How she gazes on him! the devil! 405

HORNER

Harcourt, Dorilant, look you here; this is the likeness of that dowdy he told us of, his wife. Did you ever see a lovelier creature? The rogue has reason to be jealous of his wife, since she is like him, for she would make all that see her in love with her.   410

HARCOURT

And as I remember now, she is as like him here as can be.

DORILANT

She is indeed very pretty, if she be like him.

HORNER

Very pretty? A very pretty commendation! She is a glorious creature, beautiful beyond all things I ever beheld.

386 *a guardian* (guardian Q5)
397 *this* Q1 (that Q2–5, 0)

PINCHWIFE
So, so. 415

HARCOURT
More beautiful than a poet's first mistress of imagination.

HORNER
Or another man's last mistress of flesh and blood.

MRS PINCHWIFE
Nay, now you jeer sir; pray don't jeer me.

PINCHWIFE
Come, come. (*Aside*) By heavens, she'll discover herself.

HORNER
I speak of your sister, sir. 420

PINCHWIFE
Ay, but saying she was handsome, if like him, made him
blush. (*Aside*) I am upon a rack!

HORNER
Methinks he is so handsome he should not be a man.

PINCHWIFE [*Aside*]
Oh, there 'tis out, he has discovered her. I am not able to
suffer any longer. (*To his wife*) Come, come away, I say. 425

HORNER
Nay, by your leave, sir, he shall not go yet. (*To them*)
Harcourt, Dorilant, let us torment this jealous rogue a little.

HARCOURT *and* DORILANT
How?

HORNER
I'll show you.

PINCHWIFE
Come, pray let him go, I cannot stay fooling any longer; I 430
tell you his sister stays supper for us.

HORNER
Does she? Come then, we'll all go sup with her and thee.

PINCHWIFE
No, now I think on't, having stayed so long for us, I warrant
she's gone to bed. (*Aside*) I wish she and I were well out of
their hands.—Come, I must rise early tomorrow, come. 435

HORNER
Well then, if she be gone to bed, I wish her and you a good
night. But pray, young gentleman, present my humble
service to her.

MRS PINCHWIFE
Thank you heartily, sir.

PINCHWIFE (*Aside*)
'Sdeath! she will discover herself yet in spite of me.—He is 440

something more civil to you, for your kindness to his sister, than I am, it seems.

HORNER

Tell her, dear sweet little gentleman, for all your brother there, that you have revived the love I had for her at first sight in the playhouse. 445

MRS PINCHWIFE

But did you love her indeed, and indeed?

PINCHWIFE (*Aside*)

So, so.—Away, I say.

HORNER

Nay, stay. Yes, indeed, and indeed, pray do you tell her so, and give her this kiss from me. *Kisses her*

PINCHWIFE (*Aside*)

O heavens! What do I suffer! Now 'tis too plain he knows 450 her, and yet . . .

HORNER

And this, and this . . . *Kisses her again*

MRS PINCHWIFE

What do you kiss me for? I am no woman.

PINCHWIFE (*Aside*)

So—there, 'tis out.—Come, I cannot, nor will stay any longer. 455

HORNER

Nay, they shall send your lady a kiss too. Here, Harcourt, Dorilant, will you not? *They kiss her*

PINCHWIFE (*Aside*)

How! do I suffer this? Was I not accusing another just now for this rascally patience, in permitting his wife to be kissed before his face? Ten thousand ulcers gnaw away their lips!— 460 Come, come.

HORNER

Good night, dear little gentleman; madam, goodnight; fare-well, Pinchwife. (*Apart to* HARCOURT *and* DORILANT) Did not I tell you I would raise his jealous gall?

Exeunt HORNER, HARCOURT *and* DORILANT

PINCHWIFE

So, they are gone at last! Stay, let me see first if the coach be 465 at this door. *Exit*

HORNER, HARCOURT *and* DORILANT *return*

444 *at first sight* (at the first sight Q3)
459 *this* Q1, Q4–5, 0 (his Q2–3)

HORNER
What, not gone yet? Will you be sure to do as I desired you, sweet sir?
MRS PINCHWIFE
Sweet sir, but what will you give me then?
HORNER
Anything. Come away into the next walk.   470
          Exit HORNER, *haling away* MRS PINCHWIFE
ALITHEA
Hold, hold! What d'ye do?
LUCY
Stay, stay, hold . . .
HARCOURT
Hold, madam, hold! Let him present him, he'll come presently; nay, I will never let you go till you answer my question.   475
    ALITHEA, LUCY, *struggling with* HARCOURT *and* DORILANT
LUCY
For god's sake, sir, I must follow 'em.
DORILANT
No, I have something to present you with too; you shan't follow them.
           PINCHWIFE *returns*
PINCHWIFE
Where?—how?—what's become of?—gone!—whither?
LUCY
He's only gone with the gentleman, who will give him some-   480
thing, an't please your worship.
PINCHWIFE
Something!—give him something, with a pox!—Where are they?
ALITHEA
In the next walk only, brother.
PINCHWIFE
Only, only! Where, where?   485
    Exit PINCHWIFE *and returns presently then goes out again*
HARCOURT
What's the matter with him? Why so much concerned? But dearest madam . . .
ALITHEA
Pray, let me go, sir; I have said and suffered enough already.
HARCOURT
Then you will not look upon, nor pity, my sufferings?

480 *gentleman* Q1–3 (gentlemen Q4–5, 0)

ALITHEA

    To look upon 'em, when I cannot help 'em, were cruelty not   490
    pity; therefore I will never see you more.

HARCOURT

    Let me then, madam, have my privilege of a banished lover,
    complaining or railing, and giving you but a farewell reason
    why, if you cannot condescend to marry me, you should not
    take that wretch, my rival.   495

ALITHEA

    He only, not you, since my honour is engaged so far to him,
    can give me a reason, why I should not marry him. But if he
    be true, and what I think him to me, I must be so to him.
    Your servant, sir.

HARCOURT

    Have women only constancy when 'tis a vice, and, like   500
    fortune, only true to fools?

DORILANT (*To* LUCY, *who struggles to get from him*)

    Thou sha't not stir, thou robust creature! You see I can deal
    with you, therefore you should stay the rather, and be kind.

Enter PINCHWIFE

PINCHWIFE

    Gone, gone, not to be found! quite gone! Ten thousand
    plagues go with 'em! Which way went they?   505

ALITHEA

    But into t'other walk, brother.

LUCY

    Their business will be done presently sure, an't please your
    worship; it can't be long in doing, I'm sure on't.

ALITHEA

    Are they not there?

PINCHWIFE

    No; you know where they are, you infamous wretch, eternal   510
    shame of your family, which you do not dishonour enough
    yourself, you think, but you must help her to do it too, thou
    legion of bawds!

ALITHEA

    Good brother—

PINCHWIFE

    Damned, damned sister!   515

ALITHEA

    Look you here, she's coming.

Enter MISTRESS PINCHWIFE *in man's clothes, running, with her
hat under her arm, full of oranges and dried fruit;* HORNER
following

500 *like* Q1–3 (are, like Q4–5, 0)

MRS PINCHWIFE

O dear bud, look you here what I have got, see.

PINCHWIFE (*Aside, rubbing his forehead*)

And what have I got here too, which you can't see.

MRS PINCHWIFE

The fine gentleman has given me better things yet.

PINCHWIFE

Has he so? (*Aside*) Out of breath and coloured! I must hold   520
yet.

HORNER

I have only given your little brother an orange, sir.

PINCHWIFE (*To* HORNER)

Thank you, sir. (*Aside*) You have only squeezed my orange, I
suppose, and give it me again. Yet I must have a city
patience. (*To his wife*) Come, come away.   525

MRS PINCHWIFE

Stay, till I have put up my fine things, bud.

Enter SIR JASPAR FIDGET

SIR JASPAR

O Master Horner, come, come, the ladies stay for you; your
mistress, my wife, wonders you make not more haste to her.

HORNER

I have stayed this half hour for you here, and 'tis your fault
I am not now with your wife.   530

SIR JASPAR

But pray, don't let her know so much. The truth on't is, I
was advancing a certain project to his majesty about—I'll
tell you.

HORNER

No, let's go and hear it at your house. Good night, sweet
little gentleman. One kiss more; you'll remember me now, I   535
hope.   *Kisses her*

---

522 *orange* the sexual implications here spring from the associations with
orange-wenches (Nell Gwyn was a famous one) in the theatres. Summers
cites the introduction to Duffett's *The Mock-Tempest*—

Think of thy high calling, Betty, now th'art here,
They gaze and wish, but cannot reach thy sphere,
Though ev'ry one would squeeze thy Orange there.

The lines were addressed to Betty Mackarel who had graduated from
orange-girl to actress

524–5 *city patience* the patience of a city husband who won't admit to being
cuckolded, perhaps by a fashionable gallant

R–D

DORILANT

What, Sir Jaspar, will you separate friends? He promised to
sup with us, and if you take him to your house, you'll be in
danger of our company too.

SIR JASPAR

Alas, gentlemen, my house is not fit for you; there are none   540
but civil women there, which are not for your turn. He, you
know, can bear with the society of civil women now, ha, ha,
ha! Besides, he's one of my family ... he's ... he, he, he!

DORILANT

What is he?

SIR JASPAR

Faith, my eunuch, since you'll have it, he, he, he!   545

[*Exeunt*] SIR JASPAR FIDGET *and* HORNER

DORILANT

I rather wish thou wert his, or my, cuckold. Harcourt, what a
good cuckold is lost there for want of a man to make him one!
Thee and I cannot have Horner's privilege, who can make
use of it.

HARCOURT

Ay, to poor Horner 'tis like coming to an estate at three-   550
score, when a man can't be the better for't.

PINCHWIFE

Come.

MRS PINCHWIFE

Presently, bud.

DORILANT

Come, let us go too. (*To* ALITHEA) Madam, your servant. (*To*
LUCY) Good night, strapper.   555

HARCOURT

Madam, though you will not let me have a good day or night,
I wish you one; but dare not name the other half of my wish.

ALITHEA

Good night, sir, for ever.

MRS PINCHWIFE

I don't know where to put this here, dear bud. You shall
eat it. Nay, you shall have part of the fine gentleman's good   560
things, or treat, as you call it, when we come home.

PINCHWIFE

Indeed, I deserve it, since I furnished the best part of it.

(*Strikes away the orange*)

The gallant treats, presents, and gives the ball;
But 'tis the absent cuckold, pays for all.

545 s.d. *Exeunt* ed. (Exit Q1–5, 0)
555 *strapper* lusty girl

Act IV, Scene i

In PINCHWIFE'*s house in the morning*
LUCY, ALITHEA *dressed in new clothes*

LUCY

Well, madam, now have I dressed you, and set you out with
so many ornaments, and spent upon you ounces of essence
and pulvilio; and all this for no other purpose but as people
adorn and perfume a corpse for a stinking second-hand grave
—such or as bad I think Master Sparkish's bed.   5

ALITHEA

Hold your peace.

LUCY

Nay, madam, I will ask you the reason why you would
banish poor Master Harcourt for ever from your sight? How
could you be so hard-hearted?

ALITHEA

'Twas because I was not hard-hearted.   10

LUCY

No, no; 'twas stark love and kindness, I warrant.

ALITHEA

It was so. I would see him no more because I love him.

LUCY

Hey-day, a very pretty reason!

ALITHEA

You do not understand me.

LUCY

I wish you may yourself.   15

ALITHEA

I was engaged to marry, you see, another man, whom my
justice will not suffer me to deceive or injure.

LUCY

Can there be a greater cheat or wrong done to a man than to
give him your person without your heart? I should make a
conscience of it.   20

ALITHEA

I'll retrieve it for him after I am married a while.

LUCY

The woman that marries to love better will be as much
mistaken as the wencher that marries to live better. No,
madam, marrying to increase love is like gaming to become
rich—alas, you only lose what little stock you had before.   25

2 *essence* perfume
3 *pulvilio* perfumed powder

ALITHEA

I find by your rhetoric you have been bribed to betray me.

LUCY

Only by his merit, that has bribed your heart, you see, against your word and rigid honour. But what a devil is this honour? 'Tis sure a disease in the head, like the megrim, or falling sickness, that always hurries people away to do   30 themselves mischief. Men lose their lives by it; women what's dearer to 'em, their love, the life of life.

ALITHEA

Come, pray talk you no more of honour, nor Master Harcourt. I wish the other would come to secure my fidelity to him and his right in me.   35

LUCY

You will marry him then?

ALITHEA

Certainly. I have given him already my word, and will my hand too, to make it good, when he comes.

LUCY

Well, I wish I may never stick pin more if he be not an arrant natural to t'other fine gentleman.   40

ALITHEA

I own he wants the wit of Harcourt, which I will dispense withal for another want he has, which is want of jealousy which men of wit seldom want.

LUCY

Lord, madam, what should you do with a fool to your husband? You intend to be honest, don't you? Then that   45 husbandly virtue, credulity, is thrown away upon you.

ALITHEA

He only that could suspect my virtue should have cause to do it. 'Tis Sparkish's confidence in my truth that obliges me to be so faithful to him.

LUCY

You are not sure his opinion may last.   50

ALITHEA

I am satisfied 'tis impossible for him to be jealous after the proofs I have had of him. Jealousy in a husband—heaven defend me from it! It begets a thousand plagues to a poor woman, the loss of her honour, her quiet, and her ...

LUCY

And her pleasure.   55

29 *megrim* migraine
30 *falling sickness* epilepsy
40 *natural* a fool

ALITHEA

What d'ye mean, impertinent?

LUCY

Liberty's a great pleasure, madam.

ALITHEA

I say, loss of her honour, her quiet, nay, her life sometimes;
and what's as bad almost, the loss of this town, that is, she is
sent into the country, which is the last ill usage of a husband   60
to a wife, I think.

LUCY (*Aside*)

Oh, does the wind lie there?—Then of necessity, madam,
you think a man must carry his wife into the country, if he be
wise. The country is as terrible, I find, to our young English
ladies as a monastery to those abroad. And on my virginity,   65
I think they would rather marry a London jailer than a high
sheriff of a county, since neither can stir from his employment. Formerly women of wit married fools for a great
estate, a fine seat, or the like; but now 'tis for a pretty seat
only in Lincoln's Inn Fields, St James's Fields, or the Pall   70
Mall.

Enter to them SPARKISH, *and* HARCOURT
dressed like a parson

SPARKISH

Madam, your humble servant, a happy day to you, and to us
all.

HARCOURT

Amen.

ALITHEA

Who have we here?   75

SPARKISH

My chaplain, faith. O madam, poor Harcourt remembers his
humble service to you, and in obedience to your last
commands, refrains coming into your sight.

ALITHEA

Is not that he?

SPARKISH

No, fie; no; but to show that he ne'er intended to hinder   80
our match, has sent his brother here to join our hands.
When I get a wife, I must get her a chaplain, according to
the custom. This is his brother, and my chaplain.

70-1 *Lincoln's Inn Fields* was a fashionable promenade and famous for
     assignations. *St James's Fields* is St James's Park. *Pall Mall*, originally
     built as an alley, was named after the game of pall-mail played there

ALITHEA
His brother?
LUCY (*Aside*)
And your chaplain, to preach in your pulpit, then!   85
ALITHEA
His brother!
SPARKISH
Nay, I knew you would not believe it.—I told you, sir, she
would take you for your brother Frank.
ALITHEA
Believe it!
LUCY (*Aside*)
His brother! ha, ha, he! He has a trick left still, it seems.   90
SPARKISH
Come, my dearest, pray let us go to church before the
canonical hour is past.
ALITHEA
For shame, you are abused still.
SPARKISH
By the world, 'tis strange now you are so incredulous.
ALITHEA
'Tis strange you are so credulous.   95
SPARKISH
Dearest of my life, hear me. I tell you this is Ned Harcourt
of Cambridge, by the world—you see he has a sneaking
college look. 'Tis true he's something like his brother Frank,
and they differ from each other no more than in their age,
for they were twins.   100
LUCY
Ha, ha, he!
ALITHEA
Your servant, sir; I cannot be so deceived, though you are.
But come, let's hear, how do you know what you affirm so
confidently?
SPARKISH
Why, I'll tell you all. Frank Harcourt, coming to me this   105
morning to wish me joy and present his service to you, I
asked him if he could help me to a parson. Whereupon he
told me he had a brother in town who was in orders, and he
went straight away and sent him, you see there, to me.

---

85 s.d. (*Aside*) (omit Q5)

---

92 *canonical hour* the Anglican Book of Canons dictates that a marriage
ceremony might only be performed between eight a.m. and noon

ALITHEA

Yes, Frank goes and puts on a black coat—then tells you he   110
is Ned. That's all you have for't!

SPARKISH

Pshaw, pshaw! I tell you by the same token, the midwife
put her garter about Frank's neck to know 'em asunder,
they were so like.

ALITHEA

Frank tells you this too?   115

SPARKISH

Ay, and Ned there too. Nay, they are both in a story.

ALITHEA

So, so; very foolish.

SPARKISH

Lord, if you won't believe one, you had best try him by
your chambermaid there; for chambermaids must needs
know chaplains from other men, they are so used to 'em.   120

LUCY

Let's see; nay, I'll be sworn he has the canonical smirk, and
the filthy, clammy palm of a chaplain.

ALITHEA

Well, most reverend doctor, pray let us make an end of this
fooling.

HARCOURT

With all my soul, divine, heavenly creature, when you   125
please.

116 *both in a story* both tell the same story
120 *so used* (so used so Q5)

119-20 *chambermaids ... chaplains* a running Restoration joke on the tribe
of delinquent clergy. See John Phillips, *Satyr Against Hypocrites*
(1655): 'There sits a chamber maid upon a hassock Whom th' chaplain
oft instructs without his cassock'. See also Vanbrugh's *The Relapse*
(1696), where Young Fashion says to the chaplain, Bull: 'Thou art
always for doing something in private with Nurse' (V.iii). Perhaps the
crucial formulation of this *topos* occurs in Beaumont and Fletcher's
The Scornful Lady (1610), the most consistently popular early play on the
Restoration stage according to A. C. Sprague, *Beaumont and Fletcher
on the Restoration Stage* (Cambridge, Mass., 1926; New York, 1965),
pp. 6, 123 *et passim*; but see also on its popularity *The London Stage
1660–1800*, ed. William Van Lennep, I (Carbondale, Illinois, 1965).
From his very first appearance in *The Scornful Lady* (I. i) until his final
speculations about his wedding night with Abigail, the lady's maid,
whose cry 'O Curate cure me' (IV.i) is evidently answered, Sir Roger, the
curate, provides some undeniable ammunition for those, like Collier
and Steele, who saw the stage dedicated to maligning the Church

ALITHEA

He speaks like a chaplain indeed.

SPARKISH

Why, was there not 'soul', 'divine', 'heavenly' in what he said.

ALITHEA

Once more, impertinent black coat, cease your persecution, 130
and let us have a conclusion of this ridiculous love.

HARCOURT (*Aside*)

I had forgot—I must suit my style to my coat, or I wear it in vain.

ALITHEA

I have no more patience left. Let us make once an end of
this troublesome love, I say. 135

HARCOURT

So be it, seraphic lady, when your honour shall think it meet
and convenient to do so.

SPARKISH

Gad, I'm sure none but a chaplain could speak so, I think.

ALITHEA

Let me tell you, sir, this dull trick will not serve your turn.
Though you delay our marriage, you shall not hinder it. 140

HARCOURT

Far be it from me, munificent patroness, to delay your
marriage. I desire nothing more than to marry you,
which I might do, if you yourself would; for my noble,
good-natured and thrice generous patron here would not
hinder it. 145

SPARKISH

No, poor man, not I, faith.

HARCOURT

And now, madam, let me tell you plainly, nobody else shall
marry you. By heavens, I'll die first, for I'm sure I should
die after it.

LUCY [*Aside*]

How his love has made him forget his function, as I have 150
seen it in real parsons!

ALITHEA

That was spoken like a chaplain too! Now you understand
him, I hope.

SPARKISH

Poor man, he takes it heinously to be refused. I can't blame

148-9 *die* Harcourt presumably, Wycherley certainly, intends the sexual pun
here

him, 'tis putting an indignity upon him not to be suffered.   155
But you'll pardon me, madam, it shan't be, he shall marry us.
Come away, pray, madam.

LUCY [*Aside*]

Ha, ha, he! More ado! 'Tis late.

ALITHEA

Invincible stupidity! I tell you he would marry me as your
rival, not as your chaplain.   160

SPARKISH (*Pulling her away*)

Come, come, madam.

LUCY

I pray, madam, do not refuse this reverend divine the
honour and satisfaction of marrying you—for I dare say he
has set his heart upon't, good doctor.

ALITHEA

What can you hope or design by this?   165

HARCOURT [*Aside*]

I could answer her—a reprieve, for a day only, often revokes
a hasty doom. At worst, if she will not take mercy on me
and let me marry her, I have at least the lover's second
pleasure, hindering my rival's enjoyment, though but for a
time.   170

SPARKISH

Come, madam, 'tis e'en twelve o'clock, and my mother
charged me never to be married out of the canonical hours.
Come, come! Lord, here's such a deal of modesty, I warrant,
the first day.

LUCY

Yes, an't please your worship, married women show all their   175
modesty the first day, because married men show all their
love the first day.

              Exeunt SPARKISH, ALITHEA, HARCOURT *and* LUCY

[Act IV, Scene ii]

The Scene changes to a bedchamber,
where appear PINCHWIFE, MRS PINCHWIFE

PINCHWIFE

Come, tell me, I say.

175 *an't* (and Q5)

     Scene ii s.d. PINCHWIFE, MRS PINCHWIFE Q1–3 (Pinchwife and Mrs
     Pinchwife Q4–5, 0)

MRS PINCHWIFE
  Lord! han't I told it an hundred times over?
PINCHWIFE (*Aside*)
  I would try if, in the repetition of the ungrateful tale, I
  could find her altering it in the least circumstance; for if
  her story be false, she is so too.—Come, how was't, baggage?   5
MRS PINCHWIFE
  Lord, what pleasure you take to hear it, sure!
PINCHWIFE
  No, you take more in telling it, I find. But speak—how
  was't?
MRS PINCHWIFE
  He carried me up into the house next to the Exchange.
PINCHWIFE
  So, and you two were only in the room?   10
MRS PINCHWIFE
  Yes, for he sent away a youth, that was there, for some dried
  fruit and China oranges.
PINCHWIFE
  Did he so? Damn him for it ... and for ...
MRS PINCHWIFE
  But presently came up the gentlewoman of the house.
PINCHWIFE
  Oh, 'twas well she did! But what did he do whilst the fruit   15
  came?
MRS PINCHWIFE
  He kissed me an hundred times, and told me he fancied he
  kissed my fine sister, meaning me, you know, whom he said
  he loved with all his soul, and bid me be sure to tell her so,
  and desire her to be at her window by eleven of the clock   20
  this morning, and he would walk under it at that time.
PINCHWIFE (*Aside*)
  And he was as good as his word, very punctual, a pox reward
  him for't.
MRS PINCHWIFE
  Well, and he said if you were not within, he would come up
  to her, meaning me, you know, bud, still.   25
PINCHWIFE (*Aside*)
  So—he knew her certainly. But for this confession I am

  2 *an* (a Q5)
  9 *the house* (a house Q5)
  17 *an* (a 0)
  26 *this* (his Q5)

---

  12 *China oranges* the sweet orange, supposedly from China (*citrus sinensis*).
  Pepys talks of them as a rarity in March 1665/66

obliged to her simplicity.—But what, you stood very still
when he kissed you?

MRS PINCHWIFE

Yes, I warrant you; would you have had me discover
myself?   30

PINCHWIFE

But you told me he did some beastliness to you—as you
called it. What was't?

MRS PINCHWIFE

Why, he put ...

PINCHWIFE

What?

MRS PINCHWIFE

Why, he put the tip of his tongue between my lips, and so   35
mousled me ... and I said, I'd bite it.

PINCHWIFE

An eternal canker seize it, for a dog!

MRS PINCHWIFE

Nay, you need not be so angry with him neither, for to say
truth, he has the sweetest breath I ever knew.

PINCHWIFE

The devil! You were satisfied with it then, and would do it   40
again?

MRS PINCHWIFE

Not unless he should force me.

PINCHWIFE

Force you, changeling! I tell you no woman can be forced.

MRS PINCHWIFE

Yes, but she may sure by such a one as he, for he's a proper,
goodly strong man—'tis hard, let me tell you, to resist him.   45

PINCHWIFE [Aside]

So, 'tis plain she loves him, yet she has not love enough to
make her conceal it from me. But the sight of him will
increase her aversion for me, and love for him, and that love
instruct her how to deceive me and satisfy him, all idiot that
she is. Love! 'Twas he gave women first their craft, their   50
art of deluding. Out of nature's hands they came plain, open,
silly, and fit for slaves, as she and heaven intended 'em, but
damned love ... well ... I must strangle that little monster

29 *would you* (you would Q5)
   discover ed. (discovered Q1–5, 0)
32 *called* (call 0)
36 *mousled* (musl'd Q1–5, 0) rumpled, pulled about roughly
43 *changeling* simpleton
53 *little monster* Cupid

whilst I can deal with him ... —Go, fetch pen, ink, and
paper out of the next room.   55

MRS PINCHWIFE
Yes, bud.   *Exit* MRS PINCHWIFE

PINCHWIFE (*Aside*)
Why should women have more intention in love than men?
It can only be because they have more desires, more
soliciting passions, more lust, and more of the devil.

(MRS PINCHWIFE *returns*)

Come, minx, sit down and write.   60

MRS PINCHWIFE
Ay, dear bud, but I can't do't very well.

PINCHWIFE
I wish you could not at all.

MRS PINCHWIFE
But what should I write for?

PINCHWIFE
I'll have you write a letter to your lover.

MRS PINCHWIFE
O lord, to the fine gentleman a letter!   65

PINCHWIFE
Yes, to the fine gentleman.

MRS PINCHWIFE
Lord, you do but jeer; sure you jest.

PINCHWIFE
I am not so merry, come, write as I bid you.

MRS PINCHWIFE
What, do you think I am a fool?

PINCHWIFE [*Aside*]
She's afraid I would not dictate any love to him, therefore   70
she's unwilling.—But you had best begin.

MRS PINCHWIFE
Indeed, and indeed, but I won't, so I won't!

PINCHWIFE
Why?

MRS PINCHWIFE
Because he's in town. You may send for him if you will.

PINCHWIFE
Very well, you would have him brought to you—is it come   75
to this? I say, take the pen and write, or you'll provoke me.

MRS PINCHWIFE
Lord, what d'ye make a fool of me for? Don't I know that

57 *intention* application, purpose, determination

letters are never writ but from the country to London and
from London into the country? Now, he's in town and I am
in town too; therefore I can't write to him, you know. 80
PINCHWIFE (*Aside*)
So, I am glad it is no worse; she is innocent enough yet.—
Yes, you may, when your husband bids you, write letters to
people that are in town.
MRS PINCHWIFE
Oh, may I so? Then I'm satisfied.
PINCHWIFE
Come, begin. (*Dictates*) 'Sir . . .' 85
MRS PINCHWIFE
Shan't I say 'Dear Sir'? You know one says always some-
thing more than bare 'Sir'.
PINCHWIFE
Write as I bid you, or I will write 'whore' with this pen-
knife in your face.
MRS PINCHWIFE
Nay, good bud. (*She writes*) 'Sir'. 90
PINCHWIFE
'Though I suffered last night your nauseous, loathed kisses
and embraces . . .'—Write.
MRS PINCHWIFE
Nay, why should I say so? You know I told you he had a
sweet breath.
PINCHWIFE
Write! 95
MRS PINCHWIFE
Let me but put out 'loathed'.
PINCHWIFE
Write, I say.
MRS PINCHWIFE
Well, then. *Writes*
PINCHWIFE
Let's see what you have writ. (*Takes the paper and reads*)
'Though I suffered last night your kisses and embraces'.— 100
Thou impudent creature! Where is 'nauseous' and
'loathed'?
MRS PINCHWIFE
I can't abide to write such filthy words.

82 *Yes* (yet Q3)

---

87 *bare 'Sir'* in her innocence Margery probably provokes her husband
further with the prospect of a bare sir

PINCHWIFE

Once more write as I'd have you, and question it not, or I
will spoil thy writing with this. (*Holds up the penknife*) 105
I'll stab out those eyes that cause my mischief.

MRS PINCHWIFE

O lord, I will!

PINCHWIFE

So ... so ... Let's see now! (*Reads*) 'Though I suffered last
night your nauseous, loathed kisses and embraces'.—Go
on—'Yet I would not have you presume that you shall ever 110
repeat them'.—So ...

MRS PINCHWIFE (*She writes*)

I have writ it.

PINCHWIFE

On then.—'I then concealed myself from your knowledge,
to avoid your insolencies ...'

MRS PINCHWIFE (*She writes*)

So.   115

PINCHWIFE

'The same reason, now I am out of your hands ...'

MRS PINCHWIFE (*She writes*)

So.

PINCHWIFE

'Makes me own to you my unfortunate, though innocent
frolic, of being in man's clothes ...'

MRS PINCHWIFE (*She writes*)

So.   120

PINCHWIFE

'that you may for ever more cease to pursue her, who hates
and detests you ...'   *She writes on*

MRS PINCHWIFE (*Sighs*)

So-h ...

PINCHWIFE

What, do you sigh?—'detests you ... as much as she loves
her husband and her honour'.   125

MRS PINCHWIFE

I vow, husband, he'll ne'er believe I should write such a
letter.

PINCHWIFE

What, he'd expect a kinder from you? Come now, your
name only.

MRS PINCHWIFE

What, shan't I say 'Your most faithful, humble servant till 130
death'?

131 *death* see above, note to IV. i, 148–9

PINCHWIFE

No, tormenting fiend! (*Aside*) Her style, I find, would be
very soft.—Come, wrap it up now, whilst I go fetch wax
and a candle, and write on the back side 'For Mr Horner'.
Exit PINCHWIFE

MRS PINCHWIFE

'For Mr Horner'—So, I am glad he has told me his name.   135
Dear Mr Horner! But why should I send thee such a letter
that will vex thee and make thee angry with me? ... Well, I
will not send it ... Ay, but then my husband will kill me
... for I see plainly, he won't let me love Mr Horner ...
but what care I for my husband? ... I won't, so I won't send   140
poor Mr Horner such a letter ... but then my husband ...
But oh, what if I writ at bottom, my husband made me
write it? ... Ay, but then my husband would see't ... Can
one have no shift? Ah, a London woman would have had a
hundred presently. Stay ... what if I should write a letter,   145
and wrap it up like this, and write upon't too? Ay, but then
my husband would see't ... I don't know what to do ...
But yet y'vads I'll try, so I will ... for I will not send this
letter to poor Mr Horner, come what will on't. (*She writes
and repeats what she hath writ*)

'Dear Sweet Mr Horner' ... So ... 'My husband would   150
have me send you a base, rude, unmannerly letter ... but I
won't ...' so ... 'and would have me forbid you loving me
... but I won't' ... so ... 'and would have me say to you,
I hate you poor Mr Horner ... but I won't tell a lie for him'
... there ... 'for I'm sure if you and I were in the country   155
at cards together ...' so ... 'I could not help treading on
your toe under the table ...' ... so ... 'or rubbing knees
with you, and staring in your face 'till you saw me' ... very
well ... 'and then looking down and blushing for an hour
together' ... so ... 'but I must make haste before my   160
husband come; and now he has taught me to write letters
you shall have longer ones from me, who am, dear, dear,
poor dear Mr Horner, your most humble friend, and servant
to command till death, Margery Pinchwife'.—Stay, I must
give him a hint at bottom ... so ... now wrap it up just like   165

132 *fiend* Q1, 0 (friend Q2–5)
143 *would* (will Q5)
144 *shift* expedient, device for effecting one's purpose
148 *y'vads* in faith
    send (sand Q5)
161 *come* Q1–3 (comes Q4–5, 0)
165 *hint at bottom* the postscript read by Horner at IV. iii. 278–80

t'other ... so ... now write 'For Mr Horner' ... But, oh
now, what shall I do with it? For here comes my husband.

Enter PINCHWIFE

PINCHWIFE (*Aside*)
I have been detained by a sparkish coxcomb, who pre-
tended a visit to me; but I fear 'twas to my wife.—What, have
you done?   170

MRS PINCHWIFE
Ay, ay, bud, just now.

PINCHWIFE
Let's see't. What d'ye tremble for? What, you would not
have it go?

MRS PINCHWIFE
Here. (*Aside*) No, I must not give him that, so I had been
served if I had given him this.   175

PINCHWIFE (*He opens and reads the first letter*)
Come, where's the wax and seal?

MRS PINCHWIFE (*Aside*)
Lord, what shall I do now? Nay, then, I have it.—Pray, let
me see't. Lord, you think me so arrant a fool I cannot seal a
letter? I will do't, so I will.
Snatches the letter from him, changes it for the other, seals it,
and delivers it to him

PINCHWIFE
Nay, I believe you will learn that, and other things too,   180
which I would not have you.

MRS PINCHWIFE
So. Han't I done it curiously? (*Aside*) I think I have; there's
my letter going to Mr Horner, since he'll needs have me
send letters to folks.

PINCHWIFE
'Tis very well; but I warrant, you would not have it go now?   185

MRS PINCHWIFE
Yes, indeed, but I would, bud, now.

PINCHWIFE
Well you are a good girl then. Come, let me lock you up in
your chamber till I come back. And be sure you come not
within three strides of the window when I am gone, for I
have a spy in the street.   190

182 *curiously* carefully, neatly
190 s.d. *Exit* MRS PINCHWIFE (omit Q5)

---

174 *No, I must not give him that* she almost hands him the wrong letter; a
verbal identification of visual business that would make it quite clear
to the audience that she had switched the letters

(*Exit* MRS PINCHWIFE [;] PINCHWIFE *locks the door*)
At least, 'tis fit she think so. If we do not cheat women,
they'll cheat us; and fraud may be justly used with secret
enemies, of which a wife is the most dangerous. And he that
has a handsome one to keep, and a frontier town, must
provide against treachery rather than open force. Now I have   195
secured all within I'll deal with the foe without with false
intelligence. *Holds up the letter*

Exit PINCHWIFE

[Act IV, Scene iii]

The Scene changes to HORNER's *lodging*
QUACK *and* HORNER

QUACK
Well, sir, how fadges the new design? Have you not the luck
of all your brother projectors, to deceive only yourself at
last?
HORNER
No, good Domine doctor, I deceive you, it seems, and
others too, for the grave matrons and old rigid husbands   5
think me as unfit for love as they are. But their wives,
sisters and daughters know some of 'em better things
already!
QUACK
Already!
HORNER
Already, I say. Last night I was drunk with half a dozen of   10
your civil persons, as you call 'em, and people of honour,
and so was made free of their society and dressing rooms
for ever hereafter; and am already come to the privileges of
sleeping upon their pallats, warming smocks, tying shoes
and garters, and the like, doctor, already, already, doctor.   15

191 *think* (thinks 0)
  1 *fadges* succeeds
    you not (not you Q5)
  4 *Domine* master, sir
 14 *pallats* mattresses

---

2 *projectors* schemers in the literal sense of those with schemes. Sir
Jaspar, who had earlier boasted about 'a certain project' he was advancing to his Majesty (III.ii, 532), is obviously one of the many who
proposed hare-brained schemes for one enterprise or another and whom
Swift later satirizes in *A Modern Proposal* (1729)

QUACK
    You have made use of your time, sir.
HORNER
    I tell thee, I am now no more interruption to 'em when they
    sing or talk bawdy than a little squab French page who
    speaks no English.
QUACK
    But do civil persons and women of honour drink and sing   20
    bawdy songs?
HORNER
    Oh, amongst friends, amongst friends. For your bigots in
    honour are just like those in religion. They fear the eye of the
    world more than the eye of heaven, and think there is no
    virtue but railing at vice, and no sin but giving scandal.   25
    They rail at a poor, little, kept player, and keep themselves
    some young, modest pulpit comedian to be privy to their
    sins in their closets, not to tell 'em of them in their chapels.
QUACK
    Nay, the truth on't is, priests amongst the women now have
    quite got the better of us lay confessors, physicians.   30
HORNER
    And they are rather their patients, but ...

Enter LADY FIDGET, *looking about her*

    Now we talk of women of honour, here comes one. Step
    behind the screen there, and but observe if I have not
    particular privileges with the women of reputation already,
    doctor, already.   35
                [QUACK *steps behind screen*]
LADY FIDGET
    Well, Horner, am not I a woman of honour? You see, I'm as
    good as my word.
HORNER
    And you shall see, madam, I'll not be behindhand with you
    in honour. And I'll be as good as my word too, if you please
    but to withdraw into the next room.   40
LADY FIDGET
    But first, my dear sir, you must promise to have a care of my
    dear honour.
HORNER
    If you talk a word more of your honour, you'll make me
    incapable to wrong it. To talk of honour in the mysteries of

18 *squab* chubby
27 *pulpit comedian* clergyman
29 *amongst* (among Q3)

love is like talking of heaven or the deity in an operation of   45
witchcraft, just when you are employing the devil; it makes
the charm impotent.

LADY FIDGET

Nay, fie, let us not be smutty. But you talk of mysteries and
bewitching to me—I don't understand you.

HORNER

I tell you, madam, the word 'money' in a mistress's mouth,   50
at such a nick of time, is not a more disheartening sound to a
younger brother than that of honour to an eager lover like
myself.

LADY FIDGET

But you can't blame a lady of my reputation to be chary.

HORNER

Chary! I have been chary of it already, by the report I have   55
caused of myself.

LADY FIDGET

Ay, but if you should ever let other women know that dear
secret, it would come out. Nay, you must have a great care
of your conduct, for my acquaintance are so censorious,—
oh 'tis a wicked censorious world, Mr Horner!—I say, are   60
so censorious and detracting that perhaps they'll talk to the
prejudice of my honour, though you should not let them
know the dear secret.

HORNER

Nay, madam, rather than they shall prejudice your honour,
I'll prejudice theirs; and to serve you, I'll lie with 'em all,   65
make the secret their own, and then they'll keep it! I am a
Machiavel in love, madam.

LADY FIDGET

Oh no, sir, not that way.

HORNER

Nay, the devil take me, if censorious women are to be
silenced any other way!   70

LADY FIDGET

A secret is better kept, I hope, by a single person than a
multitude. Therefore pray do not trust anybody else with it,
dear, dear Mr Horner. *Embracing him*

Enter SIR JASPAR FIDGET

SIR JASPAR

How now!

52 *younger brother* traditionally impecunious, since elder brothers inherited
72 *pray* (omit Q5)
    do not (don't Q5)   73 s.d. *Embracing him* Q1–3 (omitted Q4–5, 0)

LADY FIDGET (*Aside*)

O my husband! . . . prevented! . . . and what's almost as bad,   75
found with my arms about another man . . . that will appear
too much . . . what shall I say?—Sir Jaspar, come hither. I
am trying if Mr Horner were ticklish, and he's as ticklish as
can be. I love to torment the confounded toad. Let you and I
tickle him.   80

SIR JASPAR

No, your ladyship will tickle him better without me, I
suppose. But is this your buying china? I thought you had
been at the china house?

HORNER (*Aside*)

China house! That's my cue, I must take it.—A pox! Can't
you keep your impertinent wives at home? Some men are   85
troubled with the husbands, but I with the wives. But I'd
have you to know, since I cannot be your journeyman by
night, I will not be your drudge by day, to squire your wife
about and be your man of straw, or scarecrow, only to pies
and jays that would be nibbling at your forbidden fruit. I   90
shall shortly be the hackney gentleman-usher of the town.

SIR JASPAR (*Aside*)

He, he, he! Poor fellow, he's in the right on't, faith! To
squire women about for other folks is as ungrateful an
employment as to tell money for other folks. He, he, he!—
Ben't angry, Horner.   95

LADY FIDGET

No, 'tis I have more reason to be angry, who am left by you
to go abroad indecently alone; or, what is more indecent,
to pin myself upon such ill-bred people of your acquaintance
as this is.

SIR JASPAR

Nay, prithee, what has he done?   100

LADY FIDGET

Nay, he has done nothing.

SIR JASPAR

But what d'ye take ill, if he has done nothing?

LADY FIDGET

Ha, ha, ha! Faith, I can't but laugh, however. Why, d'ye

83 *china house* house where china was exhibited, often place of assignation
87 *journeyman* hireling who works for another
88 *drudge* slave, hack, hard toiler
89–90 *pies and jays* fops
91 *hackney* hired
93 *ungrateful* thankless
94 *tell* count

think the unmannerly toad would not come down to me to
the coach? I was fain to come up to fetch him, or go without   105
him, which I was resolved not to do; for he knows china very
well, and has himself very good, but will not let me see it lest
I should beg some. But I will find it out, and have what I
came for yet. *Exit* LADY FIDGET *and locks the door, followed*
by HORNER *to the door*

HORNER (*Apart to* LADY FIDGET)

Lock the door, madam.—So, she has got into my chamber   110
and locked me out. Oh, the impertinency of womankind!
Well, Sir Jaspar, plain dealing is a jewel. If ever you suffer
your wife to trouble me again here, she shall carry you
home a pair of horns, by my Lord Mayor she shall! Though
I cannot furnish you myself, you are sure, yet I'll find a way.   115

SIR JASPAR (*Aside*)

Ha, ha, he! At my first coming and finding her arms about
him, tickling him it seems, I was half jealous, but now I see
my folly.—He, he, he! Poor Horner.

HORNER [*Aside*]

Nay, though you laugh now, 'twill be my turn ere long.—
Oh, women, more impertinent, more cunning and more   120
mischievous than their monkeys, and to me almost as ugly.
... Now is she throwing my things about, and rifling all I
have ... but I'll get into her the back way, and so rifle her
for it.

SIR JASPAR

Ha, ha, ha! Poor angry Horner.   125

HORNER

Stay here a little, I'll ferret her out to you presently, I
warrant.

Exit HORNER *at t'other door*

SIR JASPAR

Wife! My Lady Fidget! Wife! He is coming into you the
back way!

SIR JASPAR *calls through the door to his wife;*
she answers from within

LADY FIDGET

Let him come, and welcome, which way he will.   130

SIR JASPAR

He'll catch you, and use you roughly, and be too strong for
you.

LADY FIDGET

Don't you trouble yourself, let him if he can.

104 *would not* (would Q5)
121 *monkeys* kept as pets

QUACK (*Behind*)
   This indeed I could not have believed from him, nor any but
   my own eyes.   135

                   Enter MISTRESS SQUEAMISH

SQUEAMISH
   Where's this woman-hater, this toad, this ugly, greasy, dirty
   sloven?
SIR JASPAR (*Aside*)
   So the women all will have him ugly. Methinks he is a
   comely person, but his wants make his form contemptible to
   'em; and 'tis e'en as my wife said yesterday, talking of him,   140
   that a proper handsome eunuch was as ridiculous a thing as a
   gigantic coward.
SQUEAMISH
   Sir Jaspar, your servant. Where is the odious beast?
SIR JASPAR
   He's within his chamber, with my wife; she's playing the
   wag with him.   145
SQUEAMISH
   Is she so? And he's a clownish beast, he'll give her no
   quarter, he'll play the wag with her again, let me tell you.
   Come, let's go help her . . . What, the door's locked?
SIR JASPAR
   Ay, my wife locked it.
SQUEAMISH
   Did she so? Let us break it open then.   150
SIR JASPAR
   No, no, he'll do her no hurt.
SQUEAMISH
   No. (*Aside*) But is there no other way to get into 'em?
   Whither goes this? I will disturb 'em.
                           Exit SQUEAMISH *at another door*

                   Enter OLD LADY SQUEAMISH

OLD LADY SQUEAMISH
   Where is this harlotry, this impudent baggage, this
   rambling tomrig? O Sir Jaspar, I'm glad to see you here.   155
   Did you not see my viled grandchild come in hither just
   now?
SIR JASPAR
   Yes.

---

155 *tomrig* tomboy or strumpet
156 *viled* old form of vile or perhaps, as past participle, defiled

OLD LADY SQUEAMISH

Ay, but where is she then? where is she? Lord, Sir Jaspar, I
have e'en rattled myself to pieces in pursuit of her. But can   160
you tell what she makes here? They say below, no woman
lodges here.

SIR JASPAR

No.

OLD LADY SQUEAMISH

No! What does she here then? Say, if it be not a woman's
lodging, what makes she here? But are you sure no woman   165
lodges here?

SIR JASPAR

No, nor no man neither—this is Mr Horner's lodging.

OLD LADY SQUEAMISH

Is it so, are you sure?

SIR JASPAR

Yes, yes.

OLD LADY SQUEAMISH

So—then there's no hurt in't, I hope. But where is he?   170

SIR JASPAR

He's in the next room with my wife.

OLD LADY SQUEAMISH

Nay, if you trust him with your wife, I may with my biddy.
They say he's a merry, harmless man now, e'en as harmless
a man as ever came out of Italy with a good voice, and as
pretty harmless company for a lady as a snake without his   175
teeth.

SIR JASPAR

Ay, ay, poor man.

Enter MRS SQUEAMISH

SQUEAMISH

I can't find 'em.—Oh, are you here, grandmother? I followed,
you must know, my Lady Fidget hither. 'Tis the prettiest
lodging, and I have been staring on the prettiest pictures.   180

Enter LADY FIDGET *with a piece of china in her hand, and*
HORNER *following*

172 *biddy* abbreviation for Bridget
174 *Italy with a good voice* castrato singer in Italian opera
174–5 *as pretty* (is pretty 0)

LADY FIDGET
And I have been toiling and moiling for the prettiest piece of china, my dear.

HORNER
Nay, she has been too hard for me, do what I could.

SQUEAMISH
O lord, I'll have some china too. Good Mr Horner, don't you think to give other people china, and me none. Come in with me too. 185

HORNER
Upon my honour, I have none left now.

SQUEAMISH
Nay, nay, I have known you deny your china before now, but you shan't put me off so. Come.

HORNER
This lady had the last there. 190

LADY FIDGET
Yes indeed, madam, to my certain knowledge he has no more left.

SQUEAMISH
Oh, but it may be he may have some you could not find.

LADY FIDGET
What, d'y think if he had had any left, I would not have had it too? For we women of quality never think we have china enough. 195

HORNER
Do not take it ill, I cannot make china for you all, but I will have a roll-wagon for you too, another time.

SQUEAMISH
Thank you, dear toad.

LADY FIDGET (*To* HORNER, *aside*)
What do you mean by that promise? 200

181 *moiling* labouring

182 *china* the innuendoes of the scene become most obvious here. For various *double-entendres* concerning china see the article by Aubrey Williams, 'The "Fall" of China and *The Rape of the Lock*', *PQ*, XLI (1962), reprinted in *The Rape of the Lock. A Selection of Critical Essays*, ed. John Dixon Hunt (1968), and B. Sprague Allen, *Tides in English Taste (1619–1800). A Background for the Study of Literature*, 2 vols. (Cambridge, Mass.), I., 192ff.

198 *roll-wagon* according to correspondence in *Apollo*, LXV (June 1957), p. 251 this means the 'cylindrical-bodied vases of the type frequently found in Transitional or K'ang Hsi blue-and-white'. Horner's *double-entendre* evidently refers to the shape of such vases—see photograph in *Apollo*, loc. cit.

HORNER (*Apart to* LADY FIDGET)
Alas, she has an innocent, literal understanding.
OLD LADY SQUEAMISH
Poor Mr Horner, he has enough to do to please you all, I
see.
HORNER
Ay, madam, you see how they use me.
OLD LADY SQUEAMISH
Poor gentleman, I pity you.   205
HORNER
I thank you, madam. I could never find pity but from such
reverend ladies as you are. The young ones will never spare
a man.
SQUEAMISH
Come, come, beast, and go dine with us, for we shall want a
man at ombre after dinner.   210
HORNER
That's all their use of me, madam, you see.
SQUEAMISH
Come, sloven, I'll lead you, to be sure of you.
                                   Pulls him by the cravat
OLD LADY SQUEAMISH
Alas, poor man, how she tugs him! Kiss, kiss her! That's the
way to make such nice women quiet.
HORNER
No, madam, that remedy is worse than the torment. They 215
know I dare suffer anything rather than do it.
OLD LADY SQUEAMISH
Prithee kiss her, and I'll give you her picture in little, that
you admired so last night. Prithee, do!
HORNER
Well, nothing but that could bribe me. I love a woman only
in effigy, and good painting, as much as I hate them. I'll 220
do't, for I could adore the devil well painted.
                                   Kisses MRS SQUEAMISH
SQUEAMISH
Foh! you filthy toad! Nay, now I've done jesting.
OLD LADY SQUEAMISH
Ha, ha, ha! I told you so.
SQUEAMISH
Foh! a kiss of his ...
SIR JASPAR
Has no more hurt in't than one of my spaniel's.   225

209-10 *want a man at ombre* similar pun as at II. i, 445
217 *picture in little* miniature

SQUEAMISH
    No, nor no more good neither.
QUACK (*Behind*)
    I will now believe anything he tells me.

                    Enter MR PINCHWIFE

LADY FIDGET
    O lord, here's a man! Sir Jaspar, my mask, my mask! I
    would not be seen here for the world.
SIR JASPAR
    What, not when I am with you?   230
LADY FIDGET
    No, no, my honour ... let's be gone.
SQUEAMISH
    Oh, grandmother, let us be gone. Make haste, make haste!
    I know not how he may censure us. ...
LADY FIDGET
    Be found in the lodging of anything like a man! Away!
            Exeunt SIR JASPAR, LADY FIDGET, OLD LADY SQUEAMISH,
                                                    MRS SQUEAMISH

QUACK (*Behind*)
    What's here, another cuckold? He looks like one, and none   235
    else sure have any business with him.
HORNER
    Well, what brings my dear friend hither?
PINCHWIFE
    Your impertinency.
HORNER
    My impertinency! Why, you gentlemen that have got hand-
    some wives think you have a privilege of saying anything to   240
    your friends, and are as brutish as if you were our creditors.
PINCHWIFE
    No, sir, I'll ne'er trust you any way.
HORNER
    But why not, dear Jack? Why diffide in me thou know'st so
    well?
PINCHWIFE
    Because I do know you so well.   245
HORNER
    Han't I been always thy friend, honest Jack, always ready to
    serve thee, in love or battle, before thou wert married, and
    am so still?

237 *Well*, (omit Q5)
241 *our* (omit Q5)
243 *diffide in* distrust

PINCHWIFE

I believe so. You would be my second now indeed.

HORNER

Well, then, dear Jack, why so unkind, so grum, so strange to   250
me? Come, prithee kiss me, dear rogue. Gad, I was always, I
say, and am still as much thy servant as . . .

PINCHWIFE

As I am yours, sir. What, you would send a kiss to my wife,
is that it?

HORNER

So, there 'tis. A man can't show his friendship to a married   255
man, but presently he talks of his wife to you. Prithee, let
thy wife alone, and let thee and I be all one, as we were wont.
What, thou art as shy of my kindness as a Lombard Street
alderman of a courtier's civility at Locket's.

PINCHWIFE

But you are overkind to me—as kind as if I were your   260
cuckold already. Yet I must confess you ought to be kind
and civil to me, since I am so kind, so civil to you, as to bring
you this. Look you there, sir.   *Delivers him a letter*

HORNER

What is't?

PINCHWIFE

Only a love letter, sir.   265

HORNER

From whom? . . . How! this is from your wife! (*Reads*) Hum
. . . and hum. . . .

PINCHWIFE

Even from my wife, sir. Am I not wondrous kind and civil
to you now too?—(*Aside*) But you'll not think her so!

HORNER (*Aside*)

Ha! Is this a trick of his or hers?   270

PINCHWIFE

The gentleman's surprised, I find. What, you expected a
kinder letter?

HORNER

No, faith, not I, how could I?

258 *Lombard Street* famous for goldsmiths, hence connotes wealth
259 *Locket's* fashionable restaurant
268 *I not* (not I Q5)

258-9 the point is presumably that the rich man, maybe moneylender,
 would be suspicious of civility, thinking a courtier was looking to renege
 on his repayment

PINCHWIFE

Yes, yes, I'm sure you did. A man so well made as you are, must needs be disappointed if the women declare not their 275
passion at first sight or opportunity.

HORNER (*Aside*)

But what should this mean? Stay, the postscript. (*Reads aside*) 'Be sure you love me whatsoever my husband says to the contrary, and let him not see this lest he should come home and pinch me, or kill my squirrel'.—(*Aside*) It seems 280
he knows not what the letter contains.

PINCHWIFE

Come, ne'er wonder at it so much.

HORNER

Faith, I can't help it.

PINCHWIFE

Now, I think I have deserved your infinite friendship and kindness and have showed myself sufficiently an obliging 285
friend and husband! Am I not so, to bring a letter from my wife to her gallant?

HORNER

Ay, the devil take me, art thou the most obliging, kind friend and husband in the world, ha, ha!

PINCHWIFE

Well, you may be merry, sir, but in short I must tell you, 290
sir, my honour will suffer no jesting.

HORNER

What dost thou mean?

PINCHWIFE

Does the letter want a comment? Then know, sir, though I have been so civil a husband as to bring you a letter from my wife, to let you kiss and court her to my face, I will not be a 295
cuckold, sir, I will not.

HORNER

Thou art mad with jealousy. I never saw thy wife in my life, but at the play yesterday, and I know not if it were she or no. I court her, kiss her!

PINCHWIFE

I will not be a cuckold, I say. There will be danger in 300
making me a cuckold.

HORNER

Why, wert thou not well cured of thy last clap?

PINCHWIFE

I wear a sword.

286 *so* (omit Q5)
302 *clap* venereal disease

HORNER

It should be taken from thee lest thou should'st do thyself a
mischief with it. Thou art mad, man.   305

PINCHWIFE

As mad as I am, and as merry as you are, I must have more
reason from you ere we part. I say again, though you kissed
and courted last night my wife in man's clothes, as she
confesses in her letter. . . .

HORNER (*Aside*)

Ha!   310

PINCHWIFE

Both she and I say, you must not design it again, for you
have mistaken your woman, as you have done your man.

HORNER (*Aside*)

Oh. . . . I understand something now.—Was that thy wife?
Why would'st thou not tell me 'twas she? Faith, my
freedom with her was your fault, not mine.   315

PINCHWIFE (*Aside*)

Faith, so 'twas.

HORNER

Fie! I'd never do't to a woman before her husband's face,
sure.

PINCHWIFE

But I had rather you should do't to my wife before my face
than behind my back, and that you shall never do.   320

HORNER

No—you will hinder me.

PINCHWIFE

If I would not hinder you, you see by her letter, she would.

HORNER

Well, I must e'en acquiesce then, and be contented with what
she writes.

PINCHWIFE

I'll assure you 'twas voluntarily writ. I had no hand in't, you   325
may believe me.

HORNER

I do believe thee, faith.

PINCHWIFE

And believe her too, for she's an innocent creature, has no
dissembling in her—and so fare you well, sir.

HORNER

Pray, however, present my humble service to her, and tell   330

314 *thou not* (not thou Q3)
320 *shall* (should Q5)

her I will obey her letter to a tittle, and fulfil her desires, be
what they will, or with what difficulty soever I do't, and you
shall be no more jealous of me, I warrant her and you.

PINCHWIFE

Well, then, fare you well, and play with any man's honour
but mine, kiss any man's wife but mine, and welcome.   335

Exit MR PINCHWIFE

HORNER

Ha, ha, ha! Doctor.

QUACK

It seems he has not heard the report of you, or does not
believe it.

HORNER

Ha, ha! Now, doctor, what think you?

QUACK

Pray let's see the letter ... hum ... (*Reads the letter*) 'for ...   340
dear ... love you'.

HORNER

I wonder how she could contrive it! What say'st thou to't?
'Tis an original.

QUACK

So are your cuckolds, too, originals, for they are like no other
common cuckolds, and I will henceforth believe it not im-   345
possible for you to cuckold the Grand Signior amidst his
guards of eunuchs, that I say!

HORNER

And I say for the letter, 'tis the first love letter that ever
was without flames, darts, fates, destinies, lying and dissembling in't.   350

Enter SPARKISH *pulling in* MR PINCHWIFE

SPARKISH

Come back, you are a pretty brother-in-law, neither go to
church, nor to dinner with your sister bride.

PINCHWIFE

My sister denies her marriage, and you see is gone away from
you dissatisfied.

SPARKISH

Pshaw! upon a foolish scruple that our parson was not in   355
lawful orders, and did not say all the Common Prayer. But
'tis her modesty only, I believe. But let women be never so

343 *original* unusual; *O.E.D* also gives person represented in work of art,
 hence natural, un-artificial
346 *Grand Signior* Turkish Sultan. Cf. Rochester's 'A Very Heroical Epistle
 in Answer to Ephelia', lines 32ff

modest the first day, they'll be sure to come to themselves by
night, and I shall have enough of her then. In the meantime,
Harry Horner, you must dine with me. I keep my wedding at   360
my aunt's in the Piazza.

HORNER

Thy wedding! What stale maid has lived to despair of a
husband, or what young one of a gallant?

SPARKISH

Oh, your servant, sir . . . this gentleman's sister then . . . no
stale maid.   365

HORNER

I'm sorry for't.

PINCHWIFE (*Aside*)

How comes he so concerned for her?

SPARKISH

You sorry for't? Why, do you know any ill by her?

HORNER

No, I know none but by thee. 'Tis for her sake, not yours,
and another man's sake that might have hoped, I thought.   370

SPARKISH

Another man! Another man! What is his name?

HORNER

Nay, since 'tis past he shall be nameless. (*Aside*) Poor
Harcourt! I am sorry thou hast missed her.

PINCHWIFE (*Aside*)

He seems to be much troubled at the match.

SPARKISH

Prithee tell me—nay, you shan't go, brother.   375

PINCHWIFE

I must of necessity, but I'll come to you to dinner.

Exit MR PINCHWIFE

SPARKISH

But Harry, what, have I a rival in my wife already? But with
all my heart, for he may be of use to me hereafter! For
though my hunger is now my sauce, and I can fall on heartily
without, but the time will come when a rival will be as good   380
sauce for a married man to a wife as an orange to veal.

HORNER

O thou damned rogue, thou hast set my teeth on edge with
thy orange!

SPARKISH

Then let's to dinner—there I was with you again. Come.

361 *Piazza* arcade designed by Inigo Jones near Covent Garden
376 *to dinner* (at dinner Q5)

HORNER
But who dines with thee?   385

SPARKISH
My friends and relations, my brother Pinchwife, you see, of
your acquaintance.

HORNER
And his wife?

SPARKISH
No, gad, he'll ne'er let her come amongst us good fellows.
Your stingy country coxcomb keeps his wife from his friends   390
as he does his little firkin of ale for his own drinking, and a
gentleman can't get a smack on't. But his servants, when his
back is turned, broach it at their pleasures, and dust it away,
ha, ha, ha! Gad, I am witty, I think, considering I was
married today, by the world. But come . . .   395

HORNER
No, I will not dine with you, unless you can fetch her too.

SPARKISH
Pshaw! what pleasure canst thou have with women now,
Harry?

HORNER
My eyes are not gone—I love a good prospect yet, and will
not dine with you unless she does too. Go fetch her, there-   400
fore, but do not tell her husband 'tis for my sake.

SPARKISH
Well, I'll go try what I can do. In the meantime come away
to my aunt's lodging, 'tis in the way to Pinchwife's.

HORNER
The poor woman has called for aid, and stretched forth her
hand, doctor. I cannot but help her over the pale out of the   405
briars!   *Exeunt* SPARKISH, HORNER, QUACK

[Act IV, Scene iv]

The Scene changes to PINCHWIFE's *house*
MRS PINCHWIFE *alone leaning on her elbow. A table, pen,*
ink, and paper

MRS PINCHWIFE
Well, 'tis e'en so, I have got the London disease they call
love. I am sick of my husband, and for my gallant. I have
heard this distemper called a fever, but methinks 'tis liker an
ague, for when I think of my husband I tremble and am in

391 *firkin* cask   392 *smack* (snack Q5)
393 *dust it away* toss it off

a cold sweat, and have inclinations to vomit, but when I think   5
of my gallant, dear Mr Horner, my hot fit comes and I am all
in a fever, indeed, and as in other fevers my own chamber is
tedious to me, and I would fain be removed to his, and then
methinks I should be well. Ah, poor Mr Horner! Well, I
cannot, will not stay here. Therefore I'll make an end of my   10
letter to him, which shall be a finer letter than my last,
because I have studied it like anything. Oh, sick, sick!

Takes the pen and writes

Enter MR PINCHWIFE, *who seeing her writing steals softly
behind her, and looking over her shoulder, snatches the
paper from her*

PINCHWIFE
What, writing more letters?
MRS PINCHWIFE
O lord, bud, why d'ye fright me so? *She offers to run out;
he stops her and reads*
PINCHWIFE
How's this! Nay, you shall not stir, madam. 'Dear, dear,   15
dear, Mr Horner...' Very well... I have taught you to write
letters to good purpose ... but let's see't—'First, I am to
beg your pardon for my boldness in writing to you, which
I'd have you to know I would not have done had not you said
first you loved me so extremely, which if you do, you will   20
never suffer me to lie in the arms of another man, whom I
loath, nauseate, and detest'—Now you can write these filthy
words! But what follows?—'Therefore I hope you will
speedily find some way to free me from this unfortunate
match, which was never, I assure you, of my choice, but I'm   25
afraid 'tis already too far gone. However, if you love me, as I
do you, you will try what you can do, but you must help me
away before tomorrow, or else, alas, I shall be forever out of
your reach, for I can defer no longer our ...' (*The letter
concludes*) 'Our'? What is to follow 'our'? Speak, what? Our   30
journey into the country I suppose? Oh, woman, damned
woman! And love, damned love, their old tempter! For this is
one of his miracles. In a moment he can make those blind
that could see, and those see that were blind, those dumb that
could speak, and those prattle who were dumb before—nay,   35
what is more than all, make these dough-baked, senseless,
indocile animals, women, too hard for us, their politic lords
and rulers, in a moment. But make an end of your letter and

19 *not you* (you not Q5)
37 *indocile* Weales suggests 'difficult to teach'

E

then I'll make an end of you thus, and all my plagues
together.   *Draws his sword*   40

MRS PINCHWIFE

O lord, O lord, you are such a passionate man, bud.

Enter SPARKISH

SPARKISH

How now, what's here to do?

PINCHWIFE

This fool here now!

SPARKISH

What, drawn upon your wife? You should never do that, but
at night in the dark, when you can't hurt her! This is my   45
sister-in-law, is it not? (*Pulls aside her handkerchief*) Ay, faith,
e'en our country Margery; one may know her. Come, she
and you must go dine with me; dinner's ready, come. But
where's my wife? Is she not come home yet? Where is she?

PINCHWIFE

Making you a cuckold—'tis that they all do, as soon as they   50
can.

SPARKISH

What, the wedding day? No, a wife that designs to make a
cully of her husband will be sure to let him win the first
stake of love, by the world. But come, they stay dinner for
us. Come, I'll lead down our Margery.   55

PINCHWIFE

No! ... Sir, go, we'll follow you.

SPARKISH

I will not wag without you.

PINCHWIFE [*Aside*]

This coxcomb is a sensible torment to me amidst the
greatest in the world.

SPARKISH

Come, come, Madam Margery.   60

PINCHWIFE

No, I'll lead her my way. What, would you treat your
friends with mine, for want of your own wife? (*Leads her to
t'other door and locks her in and returns*)—(*Aside*) I am contented my rage should take breath.

44 *drawn* (draw Q5)   48 *go dine* (go to dine Q5)
50 *all* (also Q5)
53 *cully* dupe, and notably a sexual dupe or cuckold
56 s.p. PINCHWIFE ed. (Mrs Pin. Q1–5, 0)
57 *wag* stir
58 *sensible* acutely felt

SPARKISH [*Aside*]
  I told Horner this.   65
PINCHWIFE
  Come now.
SPARKISH
  Lord, how shy you are of your wife! But let me tell you,
  brother, we men of wit have amongst us a saying that
  cuckolding, like the smallpox, comes with a fear, and you
  may keep your wife as much as you will out of danger of   70
  infection, but if her constitution incline her to't, she'll have
  it sooner or later, by the world, say they.
PINCHWIFE (*Aside*)
  What a thing is a cuckold, that every fool can make him
  ridiculous!—Well sir, . . . but let me advise you, now you
  are come to be concerned, because you suspect the danger,   75
  not to neglect the means to prevent it, especially when the
  greatest share of the malady will light upon your own head,
  for . . .
          Hows'e'er the kind wife's belly comes to swell
          The husband breeds for her, and first is ill.   80

Act V, Scene i

MR PINCHWIFE'*s house*
Enter MR PINCHWIFE *and* MRS PINCHWIFE
A table and candle

PINCHWIFE
  Come, take the pen and make an end of the letter, just as you
  intended. If you are false in a tittle, I shall soon perceive it,
  and punish you with this as you deserve. (*Lays his hand on
  his sword*) Write what was to follow . . . let's see. . . . 'You
  must make haste and help me away before tomorrow, or else   5
  I shall be forever out of your reach, for I can defer no
  longer our . . .' What follows 'our'?
MRS PINCHWIFE
  Must all out then, bud? (MRS PINCHWIFE *takes the pen and
  writes*) Look you there, then.
PINCHWIFE
  Let's see. . . . 'For I can defer no longer our wedding. Your 10
  slighted Alithea'.—What's the meaning of this? My sister's
  name to't? Speak, unriddle!

67 *shy* distrustful
77 *head* (heads Q5)
80 *breeds* grows cuckold's horns
    for before, and on her behalf

MRS PINCHWIFE
Yes, indeed, bud.

PINCHWIFE
But why her name to't? Speak—speak I say!

MRS PINCHWIFE
Ay, but you'll tell her then again. If you would not tell her   15
again. . . .

PINCHWIFE
I will not . . . I am stunned . . . my head turns round. Speak!

MRS PINCHWIFE
Won't you tell her indeed, and indeed?

PINCHWIFE
No, speak, I say.

MRS PINCHWIFE
She'll be angry with me, but I had rather she should be angry   20
with me than you, bud. And to tell you the truth 'twas she
made me write the letter, and taught me what I should write.

PINCHWIFE (*Aside*)
Ha! I thought the style was somewhat better than her own.
—But how could she come to you to teach you, since I had
locked you up alone?   25

MRS PINCHWIFE
Oh, through the keyhole, bud.

PINCHWIFE
But why should she make you write a letter for her to him,
since she can write herself?

MRS PINCHWIFE
Why, she said because—for I was unwilling to do it.

PINCHWIFE
Because what—because?   30

MRS PINCHWIFE
Because, lest Mr Horner should be cruel and refuse her, or
vain afterwards, and show the letter, she might disown it, the
hand not being hers.

PINCHWIFE (*Aside*)
How's this? Ha!—then I think I shall come to myself again.
This changeling could not invent this lie, but if she could,   35
why should she? She might think I should soon discover it
. . . stay . . . now I think on't too, Horner said he was sorry
she had married Sparkish, and her disowning her marriage
to me makes me think she has evaded it for Horner's sake.
Yet why should she take this course? But men in love are   40

23 s.d. (*Aside*) Q4–5, 0 (omit Q1–3)
24 *But how* Q1–3 (omit Q4–5, 0)

fools; women may well be so.—But hark you, madam, your
sister went out in the morning and I have not seen her
within since.

MRS PINCHWIFE

Alackaday, she has been crying all day above, it seems, in a
corner.   45

PINCHWIFE

Where is she? Let me speak with her.

MRS PINCHWIFE (*Aside*)

O lord, then he'll discover all!—Pray hold, bud. What, d'y
mean to discover me? She'll know I have told you then.
Pray bud, let me talk with her first.

PINCHWIFE

I must speak with her to know whether Horner ever made   50
her any promise; and whether she be married to Sparkish or
no.

MRS PINCHWIFE

Pray, dear bud, don't, till I have spoken with her and told
her that I have told you all, for she'll kill me else.

PINCHWIFE

Go then, and bid her come out to me.   55

MRS PINCHWIFE

Yes, yes, bud.

PINCHWIFE

Let me see. . . .

MRS PINCHWIFE [*Aside*]

I'll go, but she is not within to come to him. I have just got
time to know of Lucy her maid, who first set me on to work,
what lie I shall tell next, for I am e'en at my wits end!   60

Exit MRS PINCHWIFE

PINCHWIFE

Well, I resolve it; Horner shall have her. I'd rather give
my sister than lend him my wife, and such an alliance will
prevent his pretensions to my wife, sure. I'll make him of kin
to her, and then he won't care for her.

MRS PINCHWIFE *returns*

MRS PINCHWIFE

O lord, bud, I told you what anger you would make with my   65
sister.

PINCHWIFE

Won't she come hither?

MRS PINCHWIFE

No, no, alackaday, she's ashamed to look you in the face, and
she says if you go in to her, she'll run away downstairs, and

47 *he'll* (she'll 0)

shamefully go herself to Mr Horner, who has promised her 70
marriage, she says, and she will have no other, so she won't.
PINCHWIFE
Did he so—promise her marriage? Then she shall have no
other. Go tell her so, and if she will come and discourse with
me a little concerning the means, I will about it immediately.
Go! (*Exit* MRS PINCHWIFE) 75
His estate is equal to Sparkish's, and his extraction is much
better than his as his parts are. But my chief reason is I'd
rather be of kin to him by the name of brother-in-law than
that of cuckold.

Enter MRS PINCHWIFE

Well, what says she now? 80
MRS PINCHWIFE
Why, she says she would only have you lead her to Horner's
lodging—with whom she first will discourse the matter
before she talk with you, which yet she cannot do. For
alack, poor creature, she says she can't so much as look you
in the face, therefore she'll come to you in a mask. And you 85
must excuse her if she make you no answer to any question
of yours till you have brought her to Mr Horner. And if you
will not chide her nor question her she'll come out to you
immediately.
PINCHWIFE
Let her come. I will not speak a word to her, nor require a 90
word from her.
MRS PINCHWIFE
Oh, I forgot—besides, she says, she cannot look you in the
face, though through a mask, therefore would desire you to
put out the candle.
PINCHWIFE
I agree to all; let her make haste. There 'tis out. (*Puts out the* 95
candle) (*Exit* MRS PINCHWIFE)
My case is something better; I'd rather fight with Horner
for not lying with my sister than for lying with my wife, and
of the two I had rather find my sister too forward than my
wife. I expected no other from her free education, as she
calls it, and her passion for the town. Well, wife and sister 100
are names which make us expect love and duty, pleasure and

79 s.d. *Enter* MRS PINCHWIFE Q1–3 (omit Q4–5, 0)
83 *talk* Q1–3 (talks Q4–5, 0)

---

77 *his parts* abilities, but also probably a complicated irony about the
sexual parts, complicated because Pinchwife is still the only man not to
have learnt the false rumour of Horner's 'misfortune'

comfort, but we find 'em plagues and torments, and are
equally, though differently troublesome to their keeper—for
we have as much ado to get people to lie with our sisters as
keep 'em from lying with our wives!   105

Enter MRS PINCHWIFE, *masked and in hoods and scarves and a
nightgown and petticoat of* ALITHEA's *in the dark*

What, are you come, sister? Let us go then . . . but first let
me lock up my wife. Mrs Margery, where are you?
MRS PINCHWIFE
Here, bud.
PINCHWIFE
Come hither, that I may lock you up. Get you in. (*Locks the
door*)
Come, sister, where are you now?   110
MRS PINCHWIFE *gives him her hand, but when he lets her go, she
steals softly on t'other side of him, and is led away by him for his
sister Alithea*

[Act V, Scene ii]

The Scene changes to HORNER's *lodging*
QUACK, HORNER

QUACK
What, all alone? Not so much as one of your cuckolds here,
nor one of their wives! They use to take their turns with you,
as if they were to watch you.
HORNER
Yes, it often happens that a cuckold is but his wife's spy, and
is more upon family duty when he is with her gallant abroad   5
hindering his pleasure, than when he is at home with her,
playing the gallant. But the hardest duty a married woman
imposes upon a lover is keeping her husband company
always.
QUACK
And his fondness wearies you almost as soon as hers.   10
HORNER
A pox! keeping a cuckold company after you have had his
wife is as tiresome as the company of a country squire to a
witty fellow of the town, when he has got all his money.
QUACK
And as at first a man makes a friend of the husband to get the

105 s.d. *hoods and scarves* (a hood and scarf Q5)
    nightgown loose gown or wrap, usually but not necessarily worn at home

wife, so at last you are fain to fall out with the wife to be rid   15
of the husband.

HORNER

Ay, most cuckold-makers are true courtiers. When once a
poor man has cracked his credit for 'em, they can't abide to
come near him.

QUACK

But at first, to draw him in, are so sweet, so kind, so dear, just   20
as you are to Pinchwife. But what becomes of that intrigue
with his wife?

HORNER

A pox! He's as surly as an alderman that has been bit, and
since he's so coy, his wife's kindness is in vain, for she's a silly
innocent.   25

QUACK

Did she not send you a letter by him?

HORNER

Yes, but that's a riddle I have not yet solved. Allow the poor
creature to be willing, she is silly too, and he keeps her up so
close. . . .

QUACK

Yes, so close that he makes her but the more willing, and   30
adds but revenge to her love, which two, when met, seldom
fail to satisfy each other one way or other.

HORNER

What! here's the man we are talking of, I think.

Enter MR PINCHWIFE *leading in his wife, masked, muffled,
and in her sister's gown*

HORNER

Pshaw!

QUACK

Bringing his wife to you is the next thing to bringing a love   35
letter from her.

HORNER

What means this?

PINCHWIFE

The last time, you know, sir, I brought you a love letter.
Now you see a mistress I think you'll say I am a civil man to
you!   40

HORNER

Ay, the devil take me, will I say thou art the civillest man I
ever met with, and I have known some. I fancy I understand thee now better than I did the letter. But hark thee, in
thy ear . . .

41 *will I* (I will Q5)

PINCHWIFE
  What?   45
HORNER
  Nothing but the usual question, man; is she sound, on thy
  word?
PINCHWIFE
  What, you take her for a wench, and me for a pimp?
HORNER
  Pshaw! wench and pimp, paw words. I know thou art an
  honest fellow, and hast a great acquaintance amongst the   50
  ladies, and perhaps hast made love for me rather than let me
  make love to thy wife.
PINCHWIFE
  Come, sir, in short; I am for no fooling.
HORNER
  Nor I neither; therefore prithee let's see her face presently.
  Make her show, man! Art thou sure I don't know her?   55
PINCHWIFE
  I am sure you do know her.
HORNER
  A pox! why dost thou bring her to me then?
PINCHWIFE
  Because she's a relation of mine . . .
HORNER
  Is she, faith, man? Then thou art still more civil and
  obliging, dear rogue.   60
PINCHWIFE
  . . . who desired me to bring her to you.
HORNER
  Then she is obliging, dear rogue.
PINCHWIFE
  You'll make her welcome, for my sake, I hope.
HORNER
  I hope she is handsome enough to make herself welcome.
  Prithee, let her unmask.   65
PINCHWIFE
  Do you speak to her. She would never be ruled by me.
HORNER
  Madam. . . .   (MRS PINCHWIFE *whispers to* HORNER)
  She says she must speak with me in private. Withdraw,
  prithee.
PINCHWIFE (*Aside*)
  She's unwilling, it seems, I should know all her undecent   70

49 *paw* naughty
64 *she is* (she's Q5)

conduct in this business.—Well, then, I'll leave you
together, and hope when I am gone you'll agree. If not, you
and I shan't agree, sir.

HORNER [*Aside*]
What means the fool?—If she and I agree, 'tis no matter
what you and I do. *Whispers to* MRS PINCHWIFE *who makes*   75
signs with her hand for him to be gone

PINCHWIFE
In the meantime I'll fetch a parson, and find out Sparkish
and disabuse him. You would have me fetch a parson, would
you not? Well, then ... Now I think I am rid of her, and
shall have no more trouble with her. Our sisters and
daughters, like usurers' money, are safest when put out, but   80
our wives, like their writings, never safe but in our closets
under lock and key.   *Exit* MR PINCHWIFE

Enter BOY

BOY
Sir Jaspar Fidget, sir, is coming up.

[*Exit* BOY]

HORNER
Here's the trouble of a cuckold, now, we are talking of. A
pox on him! Has he not enough to do to hinder his wife's   85
sport, but he must other women's too?—Step in here,
madam.   *Exit* MRS PINCHWIFE

Enter SIR JASPAR

SIR JASPAR
My best and dearest friend.

HORNER [*Aside to* QUACK]
The old style, doctor.—Well, be short, for I am busy. What
would your impertinent wife have now?   90

SIR JASPAR
Well guessed, i'faith, for I do come from her.

HORNER
To invite me to supper? Tell her I can't come. Go.

SIR JASPAR
Nay, now you are out, faith, for my lady and the whole knot
of the virtuous gang, as they call themselves, are resolved
upon a frolic of coming to you tonight in a masquerade, and   95
are all dressed already.

75 s.d. *hand* (hands Q5)
      him Mr Pinchwife   81 *writings* deeds, documents
85 *Has he* (he has Q5)
95 *a masquerade* Q1–3 (masquerade Q4–5, 0)

HORNER

I shan't be at home.

SIR JASPAR (*Aside*)

Lord, how churlish he is to women!—Nay, prithee don't
disappoint 'em, they'll think 'tis my fault, prithee don't. I'll
send in the banquet and the fiddles. But make no noise on't,   100
for the poor virtuous rogues would not have it known for the
world, that they go a-masquerading, and they would come to
no man's ball but yours.

HORNER

Well, well—get you gone, and tell 'em, if they come, 'twill
be at the peril of their honour and yours.   105

SIR JASPAR

He, he, he! We'll trust you for that, farewell.

Exit SIR JASPAR

HORNER

> Doctor, anon, you too shall be my guest,
> But now I'm going to a private feast.

[Act V, Scene iii]

The Scene changes to the Piazza of Covent Garden
SPARKISH, PINCHWIFE

SPARKISH (*With the letter in his hand*)

But who could have thought a woman could have been false
to me? By the world, I could not have thought it.

PINCHWIFE

You were for giving and taking liberty; she has taken it only,
sir, now you find in that letter. You are a frank person, and
so is she, you see there.   5

SPARKISH

Nay, if this be her hand—for I never saw it.

PINCHWIFE

'Tis no matter whether that be her hand or no. I am sure this
hand, at her desire, led her to Mr Horner, with whom I left
her just now, to go fetch a parson to 'em, at their desire too, to
deprive you of her forever, for it seems yours was but a mock   10
marriage.

105 *honour* (honours Q5)
  1 s.d. *the letter* that written by Mrs Pinchwife that Pinchwife has unwitt-
      ingly led Sparkish to assume is from Alithea
  4 *frank* see III. ii. 333
  9 *to go fetch* (to go to fetch Q5)

SPARKISH

Indeed, she would needs have it that 'twas Harcourt himself
in a parson's habit that married us, but I'm sure he told me
'twas his brother Ned.

PINCHWIFE

Oh, there 'tis out, and you were deceived, not she, for you   15
are such a frank person—but I must be gone. You'll find her
at Mr Horner's. Go and believe your eyes.

Exit MR PINCHWIFE

SPARKISH

Nay, I'll to her, and call her as many crocodiles, sirens,
harpies, and other heathenish names as a poet would do a
mistress who had refused to hear his suit, nay more, his   20
verses on her. But stay, is not that she following a torch at
t'other end of the Piazza? And from Horner's certainly—'tis
so.

Enter ALITHEA *following a torch, and* LUCY *behind*

You are well met, madam, though you don't think so. What,
you have made a short visit to Mr Horner, but I suppose   25
you'll return to him presently. By that time the parson can
be with him.

ALITHEA

Mr Horner, and the parson, sir!

SPARKISH

Come, madam, no more dissembling, no more jilting, for I
am no more a frank person.   30

ALITHEA

How's this?

LUCY (*Aside*)

So, 'twill work, I see.

SPARKISH

Could you find out no easy country fool to abuse? None
but me, a gentleman of wit and pleasure about the town?
But it was your pride to be too hard for a man of parts, un-   35
worthy false woman! False as a friend that lends a man
money to lose. False as dice, who undo those that trust all
they have to 'em.

LUCY (*Aside*)

He has been a great bubble by his similes, as they say.

ALITHEA

You have been too merry, sir, at your wedding dinner, sure.   40

21 *a torch* a linkboy with a torch
29 *jilting* deceiving

SPARKISH
What, d'y mock me too?

ALITHEA
Or you have been deluded.

SPARKISH
By you!

ALITHEA
Let me understand you.

SPARKISH
Have you the confidence—I should call it something else,   45
since you know your guilt—to stand my just reproaches?
You did not write an impudent letter to Mr Horner, who I
find now has clubbed with you in deluding me with his aversion for women, that I might not, forsooth, suspect him for
my rival.   50

LUCY (*Aside*)
D'ye think the gentleman can be jealous now, madam?

ALITHEA
I write a letter to Mr Horner!

SPARKISH
Nay, madam, do not deny it. Your brother showed it me just
now, and told me likewise he left you at Horner's lodging
to fetch a parson to marry you to him. And I wish you joy,   55
madam, joy, joy! and to him, too, much joy! and to myself
more joy for not marrying you!

ALITHEA (*Aside*)
So I find my brother would break off the match, and I can
consent to't, since I see this gentleman can be made jealous.
—O Lucy, by his rude usage and jealousy, he makes me   60
afraid I am married to him. Art thou sure 'twas Harcourt
himself and no parson that married us?

SPARKISH
No, madam, I thank you. I suppose that was a contrivance
too of Mr Horner's and yours, to make Harcourt play the
parson. But I would, as little as you, have him one now, no, 65
not for the world, for shall I tell you another truth? I never
had any passion for you till now, for now I hate you. 'Tis true
I might have married your portion, as other men of parts of
the town do sometimes, and so your servant. And to show
my unconcernedness, I'll come to your wedding and resign   70
you with as much joy as I would a stale wench to a new cully.
Nay, with as much joy as I would after the first night, if I had
been married to you. There's for you, and so your servant,
servant.   *Exit* SPARKISH

ALITHEA

How was I deceived in a man!   75

LUCY

You'll believe, then, a fool may be made jealous now? For
that easiness in him, that suffers him to be led by a wife, will
likewise permit him to be persuaded against her by others.

ALITHEA

But marry Mr Horner! My brother does not intend it, sure.
If I thought he did, I would take thy advice and Mr   80
Harcourt for my husband. And now I wish that if there be
any over-wise woman of the town, who, like me, would
marry a fool for fortune, liberty, or title, first, that her
husband may love play, and be a cully to all the town, but her,
and suffer none but fortune to be mistress of his purse. Then,   85
if for liberty, that he may send her into the country under the
conduct of some housewifely mother-in-law. And, if for title,
may the world give 'em none but that of cuckold.

LUCY

And for her greater curse, madam, may he not deserve it.

ALITHEA

Away, impertinent!—Is not this my old Lady Lanterlu's?   90

LUCY

Yes, madam. (*Aside*) And here I hope we shall find Mr
Harcourt.   *Exeunt* ALITHEA, LUCY

[Act V, Scene iv]

The Scene changes again to HORNER's *lodging*
HORNER, LADY FIDGET, MRS DAINTY FIDGET, MRS SQUEAMISH
A table, banquet and bottles

HORNER (*Aside*)

A pox! they are come too soon ... before I have sent back
my new mistress. All I have now to do is to lock her in, that
they may not see her.

LADY FIDGET

That we may be sure of our welcome, we have brought our
entertainment with us, and are resolved to treat thee, dear   5
toad.

DAINTY

And that we may be merry to purpose, have left Sir Jaspar

90 *Lanterlu's* lanterloo or loo was a card game. See Epilogue, line 27
4 *our* (an Q5)

and my old Lady Squeamish quarrelling at home at
backgammon.

SQUEAMISH

Therefore, let us make use of our time, lest they should   10
chance to interrupt us.

LADY FIDGET

Let us sit then.

HORNER

First, that you may be private, let me lock this door and that,
and I'll wait upon you presently.

LADY FIDGET

No, sir, shut 'em only and your lips for ever, for we must   15
trust you as much as our women.

HORNER

You know all vanity's killed in me.—I have no occasion for
talking.

LADY FIDGET

Now, ladies, supposing we had drank each of us our two
bottles, let us speak the truth of our hearts.   20

DAINTY *and* SQUEAMISH

Agreed.

LADY FIDGET

By this brimmer, for truth is nowhere else to be found. (*Aside
to* HORNER) Not in thy heart, false man!

HORNER (*Aside to* LADY FIDGET)

You have found me a true man, I'm sure!

LADY FIDGET (*Aside to* HORNER)

Not every way.—But let us sit and be merry.   25

LADY FIDGET *sings*

Why should our damned tyrants oblige us to live
On the pittance of pleasure which they only give?
          We must not rejoice
          With wine and with noise.
In vain we must wake in a dull bed alone,   30
Whilst to our warm rival, the bottle, they're gone.
          Then lay aside charms
          And take up these arms.

'Tis wine only gives 'em their courage and wit
Because we live sober, to men we submit.   35
          If for beauties you'd pass
          Take a lick of the glass—

22 *brimmer* brimmer or full glass
33 *arms* glasses, as explained by a gloss in all texts

'Twill mend your complexions, and when they are gone
The best red we have is the red of the grape.
            Then, sisters, lay't on,   40
            And damn a good shape.

DAINTY
    Dear brimmer! Well, in token of our openness and plain-
    dealing, let us throw our masks over our heads.
HORNER
    So, 'twill come to the glasses anon.
SQUEAMISH
    Lovely brimmer! Let me enjoy him first.   45
LADY FIDGET
    No, I never part with a gallant till I've tried him. Dear
    brimmer, that mak'st our husbands short-sighted.
DAINTY
    And our bashful gallants bold.
SQUEAMISH
    And for want of a gallant, the butler lovely in our eyes.
    Drink, eunuch.   50
LADY FIDGET
    Drink thou representative of a husband. Damn a husband!
DAINTY
    And, as it were a husband, an old keeper.
SQUEAMISH
    And an old grandmother.
HORNER
    And an English bawd, and a French chirurgeon.
LADY FIDGET
    Ay, we have all reason to curse 'em.   55
HORNER
    For my sake, ladies?
LADY FIDGET
    No, for our own, for the first spoils all young gallants'
    industry.
DAINTY
    And the other's art makes 'em bold only with common
    women.   60
SQUEAMISH
    And rather run the hazard of the vile distemper amongst
    them than of a denial amongst us.
DAINTY
    The filthy toads choose mistresses now as they do stuffs, for
    having been fancied and worn by others.

54 *French chirurgeon* doctor for venereal disease

SQUEAMISH
For being common and cheap.   65
LADY FIDGET
Whilst women of quality, like the richer stuffs, lie untumbled
and unasked for.
HORNER
Ay, neat, and cheap, and new, often they think best.
DAINTY
No, sir, the beasts will be known by a mistress longer than
by a suit.   70
SQUEAMISH
And 'tis not for cheapness neither.
LADY FIDGET
No, for the vain fops will take up druggets and embroider
'em. But I wonder at the depraved appetites of witty men;
they use to be out of the common road and hate imitation.
Pray tell me, beast, when you were a man, why you rather   75
chose to club with a multitude in a common house for an
entertainment than to be the only guest at a good table.
HORNER
Why, faith, ceremony and expectation are unsufferable to
those that are sharp bent. People always eat with the best
stomach at an ordinary, where every man is snatching for the   80
best bit.
LADY FIDGET
Though he get a cut over the fingers . . . But I have heard
people eat most heartily of another man's meat, that is, what
they do not pay for.
HORNER
When they are sure of their welcome and freedom, for   85
ceremony in love and eating is as ridiculous as in fighting.
Falling on briskly is all should be done on those occasions.
LADY FIDGET
Well then, let me tell you, sir, there is nowhere more
freedom than in our houses, and we take freedom from a
young person as a sign of good breeding, and a person may   90
be as free as he pleases with us, as frolic, as gamesome, as
wild as he will.

72 *druggets* cheap wool fabrics
76 *common house* an ordinary or tavern restaurant; also perhaps a bawdy
house
79 *sharp bent* sharp set, hungry

---

87 *Falling on* presumably a *double-entendre* to fulfil the analogy between
eating (falling on one's food) and loving (falling on one's woman)

HORNER
Han't I heard you all declaim against wild men?

LADY FIDGET
Yes, but for all that, we think wildness in a man as desirable
a quality as in a duck or rabbit. A tame man, foh!   95

HORNER
I know not, but your reputations frightened me, as much as
your faces invited me.

LADY FIDGET
Our reputation! Lord, why should you not think that we
women make use of our reputation, as you men of yours
only to deceive the world with less suspicion? Our virtue is   100
like the statesman's religion, the Quaker's word, the gamester's oath, and the great man's honour—but to cheat those
that trust us.

SQUEAMISH
And that demureness, coyness, and modesty that you see in
our faces in the boxes at plays is as much a sign of a kind   105
woman as a vizard-mask in the pit.

DAINTY
For, I assure you, women are least masked when they have
the velvet vizard on.

LADY FIDGET
You would have found us modest women in our denials only.

SQUEAMISH
Our bashfulness is only the reflection of the men's.   110

DAINTY
We blush when they are shamefaced.

HORNER
I beg your pardon, ladies. I was deceived in you devilishly.
But why that mighty pretence to honour?

LADY FIDGET
We have told you. But sometimes 'twas for the same reason
you men pretend business often, to avoid ill company, to   115
enjoy the better and more privately those you love.

HORNER
But why would you ne'er give a friend a wink then?

LADY FIDGET
Faith, your reputation frightened us as much as ours did you,
you were so notoriously lewd.

HORNER
And you so seemingly honest.   120

101 *statesman's* (statesmen's Q5)
110 *reflection* (reflections Q5)
120 *honest* chaste

LADY FIDGET
Was that all that deterred you?

HORNER
And so expensive . . . you allow freedom, you say?

LADY FIDGET
Ay, ay.

HORNER
That I was afraid of losing my little money, as well as my little
time, both which my other pleasures required.   125

LADY FIDGET
Money, foh! You talk like a little fellow now. Do such as we
expect money?

HORNER
I beg your pardon, madam. I must confess, I have heard that
great ladies, like great merchants, set but the higher prizes
upon what they have, because they are not in necessity of   130
taking the first offer.

DAINTY
Such as we make sale of our hearts?

SQUEAMISH
We bribed for our love? Foh!

HORNER
With your pardon, ladies, I know, like great men in office,
you seem to exact flattery and attendance only from your   135
followers, but you have receivers about you, and such fees to
pay, a man is afraid to pass your grants. Besides, we must let
you win at cards, or we lose your hearts. And if you make an
assignation, 'tis at a goldsmith's, jeweller's, or china house,
where, for your honour you deposit to him, he must pawn   140
his to the punctual cit, and so paying for what you take
up, pays for what he takes up.

DAINTY
Would you not have us assured of our gallant's love?

SQUEAMISH
For love is better known by liberality than by jealousy.

129 *prizes* prices
131 *offer* (omit Q5)
136 *receivers* servants who take bribes
137 *pass your grants* accept your favours

140-2 *for your honour . . . takes up* for trusting your honour to the gallant he
     in his turn must pawn his at the goldsmith's (who will be punctual in
     asking for redemption) and, paying for your purchase, pays for taking
     up your skirt

LADY FIDGET

For one may be dissembled, the other not. (*Aside*) But my   145
jealousy can no longer be dissembled, and they are telling
ripe.—Come, here's to our gallants in waiting, whom we
must name, and I'll begin. This is my false rogue. *Claps him
on the back*

SQUEAMISH

How!

HORNER (*Aside*)

So, all will out now.   150

SQUEAMISH (*Aside to* HORNER)

Did you not tell me, 'twas for my sake only you reported
yourself no man?

DAINTY (*Aside to* HORNER)

Oh wretch! Did you not swear to me, 'twas for my love and
honour you passed for that thing you do?

HORNER

So, so.   155

LADY FIDGET

Come, speak ladies; this is my false villain.

SQUEAMISH

And mine too.

DAINTY

And mine.

HORNER

Well, then, you are all three my false rogues too, and there's
an end on't.   160

LADY FIDGET

Well, then, there's no remedy; sister sharers, let us not fall
out, but have a care of our honour. Though we get no
presents, no jewels of him, we are savers of our honour, the
jewel of most value and use, which shines yet to the world
unsuspected, though it be counterfeit.   165

HORNER

Nay, and is e'en as good as if it were true, provided the
world think so; for honour, like beauty, now, only depends
on the opinion of others.

146 *jealousy* (jealousies Q3) Maybe Q3 is trying to provide a plural antecedent for the subsequent 'they'
146-7 *they are telling ripe* the ladies are ready to be told. Q3 maybe altered
jealousy (line 146) to provide plural antecedent for 'they', so that the
meaning might be that the jealousies are ripe for telling, i.e., conspicu-
ously strong
166 *as if it were* (as 'twere Q5)

LADY FIDGET

Well, Harry Common, I hope you can be true to three.
Swear—but 'tis no purpose to require your oath for you are   170
as often forsworn as you swear to new women.

HORNER

Come, faith, madam, let us e'en pardon one another, for all
the difference I find betwixt we men and you women, we
forswear ourselves at the beginning of an amour, you as long
as it lasts.   175

Enter SIR JASPAR FIDGET *and* OLD LADY SQUEAMISH

SIR JASPAR

Oh, my Lady Fidget, was this your cunning to come to Mr
Horner without me? But you have been nowhere else, I
hope.

LADY FIDGET

No, Sir Jaspar.

OLD LADY SQUEAMISH

And you came straight hither, biddy?   180

SQUEAMISH

Yes, indeed, lady grandmother.

SIR JASPAR

'Tis well, 'tis well. I knew when once they were thoroughly
acquainted with poor Horner they'd ne'er be from him.
You may let her masquerade it with my wife and Horner, and
I warrant her reputation safe.   185

Enter BOY

BOY

Oh, sir, here's the gentleman come whom you bid me not
suffer to come up without giving you notice, with a lady, too,
and other gentlemen.

HORNER

Do you all go in there, whilst I send 'em away, and boy, do
you desire 'em to stay below till I come, which shall be   190
immediately.

Exeunt SIR JASPAR, LADY SQUEAMISH, LADY FIDGET,
MISTRESS DAINTY, SQUEAMISH

BOY

Yes, sir.   *Exit*

Exit HORNER *at t'other door, and returns with*
MISTRESS PINCHWIFE

169 *Harry Common* Horner is shared with or common to them all
170 *'tis no* Q1 ('tis to no Q2–5, 0)

HORNER
You would not take my advice to be gone home before your
husband came back; he'll now discover all. Yet pray, my
dearest, be persuaded to go home, and leave the rest to my 195
management. I'll let you down the back way.

MRS PINCHWIFE
I don't know the way home, so I don't.

HORNER
My man shall wait upon you.

MRS PINCHWIFE
No, don't you believe that I'll go at all. What, are you weary
of me already? 200

HORNER
No, my life, 'tis that I may love you long, 'tis to secure my
love, and your reputation with your husband. He'll never
receive you again else.

MRS PINCHWIFE
What care I? D'ye think to frighten me with that? I don't
intend to go to him again. You shall be my husband now. 205

HORNER
I cannot be your husband, dearest, since you are married to
him.

MRS PINCHWIFE
Oh, would you make me believe that? Don't I see every day
at London here, women leave their first husbands, and go
and live with other men as their wives? Pish, pshaw! you'd 210
make me angry, but that I love you so mainly.

HORNER
So, they are coming up.—In again, in, I hear 'em.
                    (*Exit* MISTRESS PINCHWIFE)
Well, a silly mistress is like a weak place, soon got, soon lost,
a man has scarce time for plunder. She betrays her husband
first to her gallant, and then her gallant to her husband. 215

Enter PINCHWIFE, ALITHEA, HARCOURT, SPARKISH,
LUCY *and a* PARSON

PINCHWIFE
Come, madam, 'tis not the sudden change of your dress, the
confidence of your asseverations, and your false witness
there, shall persuade me I did not bring you hither just now.
Here's my witness, who cannot deny it, since you must be

208 *would you* (you would Q5)
211 *mainly* strongly
217 *asseverations* emphatic assertions

confronted.—Mr Horner, did not I bring this lady to you   220
just now?

HORNER (*Aside*)

Now must I wrong one woman for another's sake. But that's
no new thing with me; for in these cases I am still on the
criminal's side, against the innocent.

ALITHEA

Pray speak, sir.   225

HORNER (*Aside*)

It must be so—I must be impudent and try my luck; impudence uses to be too hard for truth.

PINCHWIFE

What, you are studying an evasion, or excuse for her? Speak,
sir.

HORNER

No, faith, I am something backward only to speak in   230
women's affairs or disputes.

PINCHWIFE

She bids you speak.

ALITHEA

Ay, pray sir do, pray satisfy him.

HORNER

Then truly, you did bring that lady to me just now.

PINCHWIFE

O ho!   235

ALITHEA

How, sir!

HARCOURT

How, Horner!

ALITHEA

What mean you, sir? I always took you for a man of honour.

HORNER (*Aside*)

Ay, so much a man of honour that I must save my mistress,
I thank you, come what will on't.   240

SPARKISH

So, if I had had her, she'd have made me believe the moon
had been made of Christmas pie.

LUCY (*Aside*)

Now could I speak, if I durst, and solve the riddle, who am
the author of it.

ALITHEA

O unfortunate woman! A combination against my honour,   245
which most concerns me now, because you share in my

231 *women's* (woman's Q5)

disgrace, sir, and it is your censure which I must now suffer, that troubles me, not theirs.

HARCOURT
Madam, then have no trouble, you shall now see 'tis possible for me to love too, without being jealous. I will not only be- 250
lieve your innocence myself, but make all the world believe it. (*Apart to* HORNER) Horner, I must now be concerned for this lady's honour.

HORNER
And I must be concerned for a lady's honour too.

HARCOURT
This lady has her honour, and I will protect it. 255

HORNER
My lady has not her honour, but has given it me to keep, and I will preserve it.

HARCOURT
I understand you not.

HORNER
I would not have you.

MRS PINCHWIFE (*Peeping in behind*)
What's the matter with 'em all? 260

PINCHWIFE
Come, come, Mr Horner, no more disputing. Here's the parson; I brought him not in vain.

HARCOURT
No, sir, I'll employ him, if this lady please.

PINCHWIFE
How! what d'ye mean?

SPARKISH
Ay, what does he mean? 265

HORNER
Why, I have resigned your sister to him; he has my consent.

PINCHWIFE
But he has not mine, sir. A woman's injured honour, no more than a man's, can be repaired or satisfied by any but him that first wronged it. And you shall marry her presently, or . . . 270

Lays his hand on his sword

Enter to them MISTRESS PINCHWIFE

MRS PINCHWIFE
O lord, they'll kill poor Mr Horner! Besides he shan't marry

263 s.p. HARCOURT Q5 (Hor. Q1–4, 0) The speech obviously suits Harcourt rather than Horner. Pinchwife insists later that Horner (the 'you' of V. iv, 269) marry Alithea which he could not do as sharply if Horner had spoken this line

her whilst I stand by and look on. I'll not lose my second
husband so.

PINCHWIFE

What do I see?

ALITHEA

My sister in my clothes!   275

SPARKISH

Ha!

MRS PINCHWIFE (*To* PINCHWIFE)

Nay, pray now don't quarrel about finding work for the
parson. He shall marry me to Mr Horner, for now I believe
you have enough of me.

HORNER

Damned, damned loving changeling!   280

MRS PINCHWIFE

Pray, sister, pardon me for telling so many lies of you.

HARCOURT

I suppose the riddle is plain now.

LUCY

No, that must be my work. Good sir, hear me.
Kneels to MR PINCHWIFE, *who stands doggedly with his hat
over his eyes*

PINCHWIFE

I will never hear woman again, but make 'em all silent, thus—
Offers to draw upon his wife

HORNER

No, that must not be.   285

PINCHWIFE

You then shall go first, 'tis all one to me.
Offers to draw on HORNER; *stopped by* HARCOURT

HARCOURT

Hold!

Enter SIR JASPAR FIDGET, LADY FIDGET, LADY SQUEAMISH,
MRS DAINTY FIDGET, MRS SQUEAMISH

SIR JASPAR

What's the matter? what's the matter? pray, what's the
matter, sir? I beseech you communicate, sir.

PINCHWIFE

Why, my wife has communicated, sir, as your wife may have   290
done too, sir, if she knows him, sir.

SIR JASPAR

Pshaw! with him! ha, ha, he!

287 s.d. LADY FIDGET Q1 (omit Q2–5, 0)
290 *communicated* i.e., had sexual intercourse

PINCHWIFE

D'ye mock me, sir? A cuckold is a kind of a wild beast, have a care, sir!

SIR JASPAR

No, sure, you mock me, sir—he cuckold you! It can't be, 295
ha, ha, he! Why, I'll tell you, sir. . . . *Offers to whisper*

PINCHWIFE

I tell you again, he has whored my wife, and yours too, if he knows her, and all the women he comes near. 'Tis not his dissembling, his hypocrisy, can wheedle me.

SIR JASPAR

How! does he dissemble? Is he a hypocrite? Nay, then . . . 300
how, . . . wife . . . sister, is he an hypocrite?

OLD LADY SQUEAMISH

An hypocrite, a dissembler! Speak, young harlotry, speak, how?

SIR JASPAR

Nay, then . . . oh, my head too! . . . Oh thou libidinous lady!

OLD LADY SQUEAMISH

Oh thou harloting harlotry! Hast thou done't then? 305

SIR JASPAR

Speak, good Horner, art thou a dissembler, a rogue? Hast thou . . .?

HORNER

So . . .

LUCY (*Apart to* HORNER)

I'll fetch you off, and her too, if she will but hold her tongue.

HORNER (*Apart to* LUCY)

Canst thou? I'll give thee . . . 310

LUCY (*To* MR PINCHWIFE)

Pray, have but patience to hear me, sir, who am the un-fortunate cause of all this confusion. Your wife is innocent, I only culpable—for I put her upon telling you all these lies concerning my mistress in order to the breaking off the match between Mr Sparkish and her, to make way for Mr Harcourt. 315

300 *a hypocrite* (hypocrite Q5)
304 *my head* Q1, Q3, Q5 (my, my head Q2, Q4, 0)
   libidinous Q2–5, 0 (libinous Q1)
305 *done't then?* (omit Q4)
311 *but patience* (patience but Q5)

---

309 *she* Mrs Pinchwife. A device maybe to whet the audience's appetite for the comedy that is bound to ensue when, true to character, Margery won't hold her tongue

SPARKISH

Did you so, eternal rotten-tooth? Then it seems my mistress
was not false to me, I was only deceived by you. Brother, that
should have been, now, man of conduct, who is a frank
person now?—to bring your wife to her lover—ha!

LUCY

I assure you, sir, she came not to Mr Horner out of love,   320
for she loves him no more . . .

MRS PINCHWIFE

Hold, I told lies for you, but you shall tell none for me, for
I do love Mr Horner with all my soul and nobody shall say
me nay. Pray don't you go to make poor Mr Horner believe
to the contrary, 'tis spitefully done of you, I'm sure.   325

HORNER (*Aside to* MRS PINCHWIFE)

Peace, dear idiot!

MRS PINCHWIFE

Nay, I will not peace.

PINCHWIFE

Not till I make you.

Enter DORILANT, QUACK

DORILANT

Horner, your servant; I am the doctor's guest, he must
excuse our intrusion.   330

QUACK

But what's the matter, gentlemen? For heaven's sake, what's
the matter?

HORNER

Oh, 'tis well you are come. 'Tis a censorious world we live
in; you may have brought me a reprieve, or else I had died
for a crime I never committed, and these innocent ladies had   335
suffered with me. Therefore, pray satisfy these worthy,
honourable, jealous gentlemen . . . that . . .   *Whispers*

QUACK

Oh, I understand you; is that all?—Sir Jaspar, by heavens
and upon the word of a physician sir . . .

                               Whispers to SIR JASPAR

SIR JASPAR

Nay, I do believe you truly.—Pardon me, my virtuous lady,   340
and dear of honour.

OLD LADY SQUEAMISH

What, then all's right again?

---

333 *censorious world* perhaps a mocking reference to the same sentiment
    expressed by Lady Fidget, IV. iii, 60

SIR JASPAR
Ay, ay, and now let us satisfy him too.
They whisper with MR PINCHWIFE

PINCHWIFE
An eunuch! Pray, no fooling with me.

QUACK
I'll bring half the chirurgeons in town to swear it.   345

PINCHWIFE
They! . . . They'll swear a man that bled to death through
his wounds died of apoplexy.

QUACK
Pray hear me, sir. Why, all the town has heard the report of
him.

PINCHWIFE
But does all the town believe it?   350

QUACK
Pray enquire a little, and first of all these.

PINCHWIFE
I'm sure when I left the town he was the lewdest fellow in't.

QUACK
I tell you, sir, he has been in France since; pray ask but
these ladies and gentlemen, your friend Mr Dorilant. . . .
Gentlemen and ladies; han't you all heard the late sad report   355
of poor Mr Horner?

ALL LADIES
Ay, ay, ay.

DORILANT
Why, thou jealous fool, do'st thou doubt it? He's an arrant
French capon.

MRS PINCHWIFE
'Tis false, sir, you shall not disparage poor Mr Horner, for   360
to my certain knowledge . . .

LUCY
Oh hold!

SQUEAMISH (*Aside to* LUCY)
Stop her mouth!

LADY FIDGET (*To* PINCHWIFE)
Upon my honour, sir, 'tis as true. . . .

DAINTY
D'ye think we would have been seen in his company?   365

359 *capon* castrated cock, impotent person
364, 367 s.p. LADY FIDGET 0 (Old La. Fid. Q1–5)

346–7 duelling, though common, was illegal, so presumably doctors had to
perjure themselves about the cause of duelling fatalities

SQUEAMISH

Trust our unspotted reputations with him!

LADY FIDGET (*Aside to* HORNER)

This you get, and we too, by trusting your secret to a fool.

HORNER

Peace, madam. (*Aside to* QUACK) Well, doctor, is not this a
good design, that carries a man on unsuspected, and brings
him off safe?   370

PINCHWIFE (*Aside*)

Well, if this were true, but my wife . . .

DORILANT *whispers with* MRS PINCHWIFE

ALITHEA

Come, brother, your wife is yet innocent you see. But have a
care of too strong an imagination, lest like an over-concerned,
timorous gamester, by fancying an unlucky cast, it should
come. Women and fortune are truest still to those that trust   375
'em.

LUCY

And any wild thing grows but the more fierce and hungry for
being kept up, and more dangerous to the keeper.

ALITHEA

There's doctrine for all husbands, Mr Harcourt.

HARCOURT

I edify, madam, so much that I am impatient till I am one.   380

DORILANT

And I edify so much by example I will never be one.

SPARKISH

And because I will not disparage my parts I'll ne'er be one.

HORNER

And I, alas, can't be one.

PINCHWIFE

But I must be one—against my will, to a country wife, with a
country murrain to me.   385

MRS PINCHWIFE (*Aside*)

And I must be a country wife still too, I find, for I can't, like
a city one, be rid of my musty husband and do what I list.

HORNER

Now, sir, I must pronounce your wife innocent, though I
blush whilst I do it, and I am the only man by her now
exposed to shame, which I will straight drown in wine, as   390

381 *edify* gain instruction
382 s.p. SPARKISH Q5 (Eew. Q1)
385 *murrain* cattle plague
389 *whilst* (while Q5)

you shall your suspicion, and the ladies' troubles we'll divert
with a ballet. Doctor, where are your maskers?

LUCY

Indeed, she's innocent, sir, I am her witness. And her end of
coming out was but to see her sister's wedding, and what
she has said to your face of her love to Mr Horner was but   395
the usual innocent revenge on a husband's jealousy—was it
not, madam? Speak.

MRS PINCHWIFE (*Aside to* LUCY *and* HORNER)

Since you'll have me tell more lies.—Yes, indeed, bud.

PINCHWIFE

For my own sake fain I would all believe;
Cuckolds, like lovers, should themselves deceive   400
But ... (*Sighs*)
His honour is least safe, too late I find,
Who trusts it with a foolish wife or friend.
            A dance of cuckolds

HORNER

Vain fops, but court, and dress, and keep a pother
To pass for women's men with one another;   405
But he who aims by women to be prized,
First by the men, you see, must be despised!

404 *pother* turmoil

───────────────────────────

403 s.d. *dance of cuckolds* as Weales rightly maintains, if this dance is to have
any meaning for an audience, it must be to well-known and appropriate
music. He suggests the tune, 'Cuckolds All a Row', to which Pepys
saw King Charles II dancing in December 1662, and which was
available in five editions of John Playford's *The Dancing Master* between
1652 and 1675

EPILOGUE
Spoken by Mrs Knep

Now, you the vigorous, who dally here
O'er vizard mask in public domineer,
And what you'd do to her if in place where;
Nay, have the confidence to cry 'come out!'
Yet when she says 'Lead on' you are not stout   5
But to your well-dressed brother straight turn round
And cry 'Pox on her, Ned, she can't be found!'
Then slink away, a fresh one to engage,
With so much seeming heat and loving rage,
You'd frighten listening actress on the stage,   10
Till she at last has seen you huffing come,
And talk of keeping in the tiring-room,
Yet cannot be provoked to lead her home.
Next, you Falstaffs of fifty, who beset
Your buckram maidenheads, which your friends get   15
And whilst to them you of achievement boast
They share the booty, and laugh at your cost.
In fine, you essenced boys, both old and young,
Who would be thought so eager, brisk, and strong,
Yet do the ladies, not their husbands, wrong;   20
Whose purses for your manhood make excuse,
And keep your Flanders mares for show, not use;
Encouraged by our woman's man today
At Horner's part may vainly think to play;
And may intrigues so bashfully disown   25
That they may doubted be by few or none;
May kiss the cards at picquet, ombre, loo,
And so be thought to kiss the lady too;
But, gallants, have a care, faith, what you do.

Epilogue *Mrs Knep* Q2–5, 0 (Mr Hart Q1) Obviously should be spoken by
an actress

15 *buckram* stiff. But also, continuing the Falstaff reference, it may mean
'illusionary', like the buckram rogues Falstaff pretends to have fought
in 1 *Henry IV*, II. iv.
18 *essenced boys* perfumed boys (or, perhaps, boys only 'in essence')
22 *Flanders mares* Flemish horses were imported mainly for breeding, which
makes the sarcasm stronger
27 *picquet* another popular card game, like ombre and loo
28 *thought* Q1 (taught Q2–5, 0)

133

The world, which to no man his due will give,   30
You by experience know you can deceive.
And men may still believe you vigorous,
But then we women—there's no coz'ning us!

Printed in Great Britain by Cox & Wyman Ltd.,
London, Reading and Fakenham